|| | | ||||||| | |||| ||| || |||| |||
I0164731

STRENGTH TO ENDURE

A compilation of prayers, confessions, and poetry from me as directed by God

© 2013 Sharan Fifer

All rights reserved, including the right to reproduce this book or portion thereof in any form whatsoever without the expressed, written consent of the author, except for the use of brief quotations in a book review.

Published by Primedia E-launch LLC
Manufactured in the United States of America
ISBN 10 0615853501
ISBN 13 is 9780615853505

Cover design by Salient Success Marketing, LLC
Edited by Writer's Ease, Robin L. Burns
Interior Design by Offsite Solutions

Scripture quotations are from the following sources: The New Century Version® Copyright© 2005 by Thomas Nelson, Inc. The Holy Bible, New International Version®. Copyright© 1973, 1978, 1984 by International Bible Society. Used by permission of Zondervan Publishing House. All rights reserved. The Holy Bible, New Living Translation®. Copyright© 1996. Used by permission of Tyndale House Publishers, Inc., Wheaton, Il 60189. All rights reserved. The World English Bible is in the Public Domain (no copyright). Weymouth New Testament in Modern Speech, Third Edition 1913. Public Domain. Copy freely. The King James Version. Public Domain. The New King James Version®. Copyright© 1982 by Thomas Nelson, Inc. Used by permission. All rights reserved.

The name satan and other related names appear without capitalization. We chose not to acknowledge him even to the point of violating grammatical rules.

STRENGTH TO ENDURE

*A compilation of prayers, confessions, and poetry from
me as directed by God*

Sharan Fifer

DEDICATION

To God for Jesus Christ, my Redeemer, my Savior who delivered me from the hands of satan and set my soul free, I present this book back unto You for Kingdom building.

But those who wait on the LORD
shall renew *their* Strength to Endure;
Isaiah 40:31 NJKV [emphasis added]

Prayer for My Readers

Dear Most Gracious and Heavenly Father,

I pray that You, O' God touch the readers of this book right now with Your Holy Spirit. I pray that as they pray these prayers and meditate on Your Word, their worries, troubles, and anxieties will flee and be replaced by peace and assurance that You know what You are doing. I ask that You birth in them a desire to draw closer to You. I pray that through Your angels and the workings of Your Holy Spirit, You will give them direction and steps to live a holy life. Grant each reader the ability to hear Your audible voice. I pray that they develop a thirst with a real longing to spend more time in prayer getting to know You and Your plans and purposes for their lives. I ask that You bless them, keep them, and make Your face shine upon them and give them peace, prosperity, and power. In the Mighty Name of Jesus.

Your daughter,
Sharan

Contents

Preface 7

Introduction 11

The People: Who Should We Pray For? 15

The Purpose: Why Pray? 19

The Predicament: What to Pray? 24

The Power: Praying Effectively 27

The Provision: Receive the Promise 31

The Place and Time 35

The Posture: Positioning Yourself 38

The Problem: Not Seeing Results 44

The Privilege: Praise 48

Names of God 53

The Prayers 59

Sin 60

Cleansing 62

The Blood of Jesus 64

Anxiety and Worry 65

Jealousy and Envy 67

Sickness 69

Marriage 72

Forgiveness 76

Faith 78

Purity and Holiness 79

Patience and Waiting.. 82

Addictions and Temptations 84

Self-Esteem 87

Children 90

Protection 94

Authority and Identity 96

Government 98

Neighborhood 99

Setbacks and Disappointments 101

Obedience 103

Making Tough Decisions 105

Finances 107

Confusion and Depression 112

Love 114

God's House 116

Relationships 126

Favor 127

My Words 129

Success 130

Salvation 133

Reference 135

Acknowledgements 136

About the Author 138

Book Recommendations 140

Preface

God desires to bring forth a generation in this hour that will, *"...humble themselves and pray."* When the Lord finds a generation that will dedicate themselves to prayer, He says that He will answer them and show them great and mighty things that have never been heard of or revealed.

This book was birthed out of my desire to be a part of that generation that God is seeking. It is composed of my personal prayers, confessions and poetry. To some, this book may seem like just another random book of prayers, but to me, this book is my heart. I asked God what He wanted to say to the readers and then I prayerfully selected the material from this book. That is why it is subtitled, "From Me as Directed by God." If you have been feeling down, defeated, discouraged or disillusioned by life's trials and temptations, this book will give you the *Strength to Endure* any situation, circumstance, or condition until change comes because it is based on God's Word.

Cast your burden upon the LORD and He will sustain you; He will never allow the righteous to be shaken.-Psalm 55:22

Ever since I can remember, my mother has always taught me the importance of prayer. She knew that prayer was the key to manifesting any and everything in life. I soon experienced

God's healing power first hand. When I was thirteen, I had a large lump on the back of my neck. The doctors didn't know what it was. I was told by one doctor that it would never go away, but if it began to bother me, he would remove it. But he would only remove it if it became unbearable. There was never any physical pain; however, the pain of being teased day after day was overwhelming. My mother continued to pray and taught me how to pray for my own healing.

> See, without a close personal relationship with God, we don't understand His plan, and our hearts are full of fear.

Soon the lump began to shrink before everyone's eyes. Glory to God! As I grew older, I continued to pray the prayers that my mother instilled in me as a child, but I never really grew or developed in that area and never formed a real relationship with God. I saw prayer as a ritual and my *get-out-of-jail-free* or *break-in-case of emergency* card. Even though I would pray about my situations, I was still stricken with fear. See, without a close personal relationship with God, we don't understand His plan, and our hearts are full of fear. Prayer becomes a ritual. But when I really began to have a real relationship and grow in Christ, it challenged me to elevate my prayer life. I began praying and seeking God more and more for answers, direction, and strength.

The problem was that I would attend worship and prayer services and become intimidated by the prayers of others. The prayers were so eloquent and seemed to roll off the speaker's tongue like silk. Where I was from, prayers were prewritten and all I had to do was read. But these people were rolling them off the top of their head and they seemed to have power. I felt like a baby. After all, I was a 30-something year old mother that still prayed, "Lord lay me down to sleep..." before I went to bed at night.

Jesus disciples asked, "Lord teach us to pray." –Luke 11:1

I wanted to pray with power too, so I began to pray and ask God to grace me with that same gift. I didn't know then, but now I know, to be careful what you ask God for. One day I was called upon to pray at a meeting. I cried and flat out said, "No!" I couldn't do it. I didn't know how. Then the ladies at this meeting began to surround me and tell me their testimonies of prayer. Many started out their spiritual journey just like me. Then First Lady Burns said something that I would never forget. She said, "Prayer is just talking to God-a personal experience and intimate connection with Him. He cares more about sincerity." She told me to read my Bible and search scriptures for what I was seeking God for. Now I understand that the more the Word of God is deposited within us, the more spontaneous our prayers will become. When you know the scriptures, you know

9

the Will of God. Knowing God's Will helps us to effectively pray prayers that are pleasing to God. What I thought was so eloquent was simply the Word of God.

I know there are others who are experiencing the same thing. Well, you don't have to worry or feel ashamed anymore. You see, praying is a learnable skill. It's not enough to read this book. You will never learn by simply reading this book. You will never learn by simply reading the Bible. An effective prayer life is learned and developed through practice. I know this book will help you. It contains guides and models of prayers and confessions. You can use them as is, but I challenge you to make them your own. You are free to change the words around, add your name, or your situation. Again, make them your own. I believe as you continue with these prayers and remain in God's Word; the Holy Spirit will help you develop your own style as you yield to His guidance as He gives you what to pray. Let this book serve as your introductory course and the Holy Spirit will lead you in the master course.

Introduction

Prayer is a powerful weapon that connects us to God and gets Him involved in our lives. God invites us to pray. Someone once said, "A believer without prayer is a believer without power". Dr. Martin Luther King, Jr. was quoted as saying, "To be a Christian without prayer is no more possible than to be alive without breathing." Wow! We cannot truly function and live the way God intended without a prayer life...communication with God. God wants us to cast our cares upon Him for it shows our reliance and trust in Him. The word says that we can come to Him boldly and find mercy and grace.

Many Christians only see prayer as a ritual they say before meals and bedtime. And still others see it as a *get-out-of-jail- free* card or a *S.O.S.* when distressed or in trouble. Our misconceptions about prayer have

> "A believer without prayer is a believer without power".

clouded the image of true prayer. James S. Stewart, a great missionary statesman of the 20th century, wrote, "The man who does not pray, who not have even five minutes a day, in his own rooms, face to face with God and heart to heart with Christ, is simply playing with his soul." He goes on to say, "I am saying that without prayer there is no Christian life possible that is worthy of the name because it is down in the channel of prayer that the power of God gets into a man."

Here is what I have found to be one of the greatest issues. As new Christians, we are told to "Read your bible and don't forget to pray." Reading my bible was simple enough. I am a pretty proficient reader; however, praying posed a problem. I didn't know how to pray. I sat through new members' class, Sunday school, and a host of other classes and church services where this was echoed, but no one bothered to teach me how to pray. I didn't dare ask. "Don't forget to pray" seemed like a simple enough request to those giving the command; I didn't want to be seen as incompetent or unspiritual. That brings me to the goal of this book. The goal of this book is to make prayer so simple and so accessible that you will make it a regular part of your life. My desire is to present you with brief lessons and models to use as your springboard to an effective prayer life. Why? Because with the power of prayer you can overcome enemies (Psalm 6:9-10), conquer death (2 Kings 4:3-36), receive healing (James 5:14-15), and defeat demons (Mark 9:29). God, through prayer, opens eyes, changes hearts, heals wounds, and grants wisdom (James 1:5). Why? Because God is our Father; He is our Creator and He yearns to hear our voice. Why? Because we love Him. How odd is it to be in love with someone and never communicate with that person. I cannot imagine a marriage in which the husband and wife rarely spoke and when they did speak, they would be too thrilled if the only conversation that they had was about money or when they needed to be rescued from a desperate situation. The marriage probably would not last too long. Prayer is like talking to a spouse or a good friend. It is speaking and listening to someone we trust with our concerns and secrets.

As Believers, we can receive spiritual strength to continue on life's journey until change comes. I also believe that through prayer and confession, we can change the course of events. Historically, prayer has transformed lives, churches, cities, and nations. God can do anything, but He chooses to partner with us to manifest His Glory here on earth.

What are some things that you could have prevented in life, if only you understood the importance of prayer and took the time to pray? Could your marriage still be intact? Could 911, Hurricane Katrina or Sandy have been avoided? Could the Jezebel or Python Spirit been crushed at your church? Could your children be completely sold out to God? Just imagine...the possibilities are endless.

When all hell broke loose in my life, I used to run around trying to put out fires all around me. I since learned to pray preventive prayers beforehand. Did all trouble cease? No, however, there were a lot of things that were prevented as a result. In many cases, God gave me a strategic plan to help me through these times.

Sadly, many Christians live their lives in complete fear of their present and future. They seek out psychics, Ouija boards, horoscopes and other satanic devices. We must wake up and open our eyes to what is going on around us.

Awake you who sleep, and arise from among the dead and the Messiah will illuminate you. –Ephesians 5:14

THE PEOPLE

WHO SHOULD WE PRAY FOR?

I often hear people say that they don't know who to pray for or what to pray. God tells us to pray for others. Sometimes, the Holy Spirit puts someone in our thoughts. Several times, I've had people pop into my mind in the middle of the night, or as I'm going about my day. I've learned to make sure to pray for them when that happens, we never know right at that moment what that person is going through, but God does and He has a purpose in putting that person on your mind.

I have established areas in which I pray. Following, is not an exhausted list, but it will get you started.

MYSELF- Originally, I listed this one last. I always thought that I should pray for the needs of others before I prayed for myself or my needs. I felt it was selfish. Then God gave me this example: When you are in a plane crash and you have a young child, they tell you to put the oxygen mask on yourself first before the child. Why, because you can't help them if you are unconscious or dead. Your first priority is to keep yourself awake and alert AND THEN help the kids. The same holds true in prayer. If you are not prayed up, how can you effectively pray for someone else? When we pray and receive God's direction and guidance, we are awake and alert to discern what is happening in the spiritual realm. I have heard people say that it is selfish to pray for oneself. This is untrue. Jesus prayed for himself (Matthew 26:39). I ask God to let His will be done in my life. I ask Him for more influence to greater impact the kingdom. I ask for finances and resources to be a blessing to others and to build the kingdom. We must pray for ourselves so that God may be glorified through us and that we are free to hear from Him and gain wisdom.

God appeared to Solomon and said, "What do you want? Ask, and I will give it to you!" Solomon replied to God... "Give me the wisdom and knowledge to lead properly..."
2 Chronicles 1:7, 10-12.

Avoid selfish prayers, prayers motivated by self, ambition or the desire for self-indulgence, self-recognition, or self-promotion. Such prayers are from the "flesh" and not from the Spirit, and Jesus says that the things of the spirit are Spirit (John 3:6)

FAMILY-I pray out loud with and for my spouse and confess the Word of God over my children daily. I pray for my mother and my siblings- especially those who do not know Christ.

CHURCH-I pray for my Pastor and his family. REMEMBER: If the enemy can't get to the pastor, he'll focus on his family. I pray for ministers and other leaders in my church. 1 Thessalonians 3:9-13. I confess the Word of God over my church and its members.

17

WORKPLACE- Speak blessings over your boss (do this even if he/she is a tyrant). I confess the Word of God over my work area and co-workers. I pray for the success of the organization in which I work (If they are not a success, you won't have a job).

YOUR CITY, THE NATIONS, LEADERS & OTHER GOVERNMENT OFFICIALS-Particularly for nations that are oppressed and have no religious freedom. I pray that God send laborers to deliver His Word to the lost. 1Timothy 2:1-2

OUR ENEMIES & THOSE WHO PERSECUTE ME-Yes, you read it correctly. I regularly pray for my enemies. In fact, the Bible exhorts us in Matthew 5:44 to do just that. Not for their destruction, but I speak blessings over their lives.

THE PURPOSE

"More things are wrought by prayer than
this world dreams of." –Alfred Lord Tennyson

WHY PRAY?

God releases His will and manifests His presence in the earth through prayer. My Pastor always says, "if God is going to do something in the earth, He's going to do it through you and me."

> *Your adversary, the devil, prowls around like a roaring lion, seeking someone to devour.* -1 Peter 5:8

According to 1 Samuel 12:23, prayerlessness is a sin. The enemy is working overtime to keep people from praying. I am going to just lay it out there...satan hates you. Don't get confused. It's not about you. He hates the God in you. His assignment is to kill, steal, and destroy you. He does not fight fair. He will ruthlessly employ any scheme or method to help him reach his goal. Satan is not playing games. He is dead serious about his calling, unlike many Christians.

> You cannot afford to leave your present and future to the pastor or the intercessory prayer team at your church.

There are weapons being aimed at you from every direction at this very moment. You can go to church every Sunday, obey every scripture, give to the poor, be a born-again believer, sing, shout and cry and do whatever other religious act you can think to do. You can do everything you think is right, but if you do not pray, you will not be able to effectively fight. You cannot afford to leave your present and future to your pastor or the intercessory prayer team at your church. No one has more authority to pray for you than YOU. You need to be aware of satan's wiles, and frustrate his every move. How? You must learn to pray for yourself, your family, and everything concerning you. You must learn to confess the Word of God over your situation, circumstance, and condition.

But I am afraid that your minds will be led away from your true and pure following of Christ just as Eve was tricked by the snake with his evil ways.-2 Corinthians 11:3

Anyone is susceptible to satan's attacks. However, many Christians underestimate satan. They believe because they live godly lives, satan will not attack them. It can be a deadly mistake to underestimate one's opponent. Don't be a fool, living in denial. The Bible says that we are not to be ignorant of satan's devices. Many are maneuvering through life haphazardly while satan is tearing their lives apart. His first tactic is to surround us and cut off our supplies. It is his desire to get us out of the Word, out of fellowship, and out of prayer. Just look at how many Believers are deceived, suffering from church hurt, bitterness, greed, and are going through divorces. As a matter of fact, Christians divorce at roughly the same rate as the world.

So, if you think you are standing firm, be careful that you don't fall!-1 Corinthians 10:12

Evaluate your life. How is satan attacking you? If you believe he is not attacking you, remember everything happens in the unseen spirit realm before it is manifested in the seen or the earth realm. This realm is very real. Yes, there is an unseen realm in the spirit. If you find yourself losing the desire to go to church or to be around other Christians - watch out there is a war going on in the spirit realm seeking control and power! If your prayer life is dwindling or non-existent, and your consistent study of the Word is lacking - be careful! Stay alert! During these times you need strategies that only God is able to give. Yes, you are in a fierce battle, but the fight is fixed in your favor. satan is a defeated foe. You are more than a conqueror. Not just a conqueror, but more than a conqueror! Again, a Believer without prayer is a Believer without power. The only power that satan has is the power that we appropriate to him when we do not pray. Through our prayers we can influence the spirit realm and bring about change impacting the world. Your prayers, like David's, Daniel's and Esther's can change the course of history. There are countless others who, through prayer, accomplished greatness and saw the events in their lives changed.

- What if you could stop your divorce and reunite with your spouse?
- What if you could release your loved one from the trap of substance abuse?

- What if you could stop your son or daughter from making life altering decisions that cause them to stray away from God?
- What if you could live in supernatural, overflowing abundance?
- What if you could have stopped Hurricane Katrina or 911?

Guess what? You have the power to do those things and MORE. Yes, you can be that modern day person that brings about change in the earth. You are God's voice, His feet, and His hands in the earth.

"Elias was a man subject to like passions as we are, and he prayed earnestly that it might not rain; and it rained not on the earth by the space of three years and six months."-James 5:27

In this day and age, the way that you've been living and the prayers that you have been praying are not enough for what lies ahead. Let's go deeper! God is calling us higher!

THE PREDICAMENT

WHAT TO PRAY?

Sometimes, there are things that we go through in life that just seem too big for us to handle. We feel like it's more than we can bear. Have you ever been there? There have been times that I felt lost, overwhelmed, discouraged, and even confused. I did not know what to do or even what to think, much less what to pray. It was at times like these that the Holy Spirit stepped in to help. It was when I cried out, "God help!" and yielded myself to Him, that He began to take over my prayers. Other times, I just mentally be still and allow the Holy Spirit to guide me. Other times, I just mentally be still and allow the Holy Spirit to guide my words and take control of my tongue. I know this may sound weird, but the Bible speaks of praying in-the-Spirit (tongues).

"Likewise the Spirit helps us in our weakness. For we do not know what to pray for as we ought, but the Spirit himself intercedes for us with groanings too deep for words."-Romans 8:26.

I urge you today to be still and yield yourself to the Holy Spirit and let Him put it upon your heart as to what to pray and how to pray. The Holy Spirit wants to disclose God's will and strategies to us. Even when praying for others, we do not need to know all the details and specifics. Romans 8:26-27 tells us,

"Likewise the Spirit also helps in our weaknesses. For we do not know what we should pray for as we ought, but the Spirit Himself makes intercession for us with groanings which cannot be uttered. Now He who searches the hearts knows what the

25

mind of the Spirit is, because He makes intercession for the saints according to the will of God." I ask for God's will to be done in the situation.

"In praying in-the-Spirit, the believer lets the Holy Spirit make the words flow from their own heart spontaneously after yielding to Him. The words just flow in power. The degree to which this happens depends upon the degree of tug and yieldedness. It must be practiced. Thus, it should be your goal to let the Holy Spirit pray through you and with you, in your own language, and to seek to let Him make the words arise from your heart, directed upward to the Lord. You let Him lead the prayer." (Zumpano, 1999)

THE POWER

"Prayer is not getting man's will done in heaven, but getting God's will done on earth. It is not overcoming God's reluctance but laying hold of God's willingness."
–Richard C. Trench

PRAYING EFFECTIVELY

Prayer is a weapon. For any weapon to be powerful it must be used effectively. In order to use it effectively, you must understand how it functions before you use it. With that being said, we are not to use prayer to try and get God to do what we want done.

"Lord, if it's your will."

Have you ever heard this prayer so often used by Christians? Effective prayers have their foundation in the Word of God. When you know the Word of God, you know the will of God. No more wondering if it is His will. When you know the will of God, you know what to pray and you can be assured that your prayers are answered.

Go with me for a minute to John 18:11.

Jesus rebuked Peter saying, "Put your sword back in its scabbard; am I not to drink the cup that the Father has given me?" Here, we see Jesus chastising Peter in the Garden when Peter drew his sword to defend his Master against the Temple guards and Roman soldiers sent to arrest Jesus.

This scripture clearly shows us that Jesus knew it was God's will... *"Am I not to drink the cup that the Father has given me?"*

That is why He was able to confidently declare, *"Yet I want your will to be done, not mine."*

> When we go to God in prayer, we go to bring ourselves in alignment with His heart and His Will.

Not yet convinced?

Let's take a look at the Gospels. Matthew 16:21, 17:23, 20:19; Mark 8:31, 9:31, 10:34; Luke 9:22, 18:33, have Jesus predicting his resurrection as well as his death, even as he was on his final journey to Jerusalem. In John, the equivalent is Jesus' confident "I am the resurrection and the life" (11:25) as well as the more enigmatic "Destroy this temple, and in three days I will raise it up." (2:19). (Kirk, 2008). He knew God's will. You can know His will as well. Start now diving into the Word of God so that you may know His will. No matter the situation or need, there is an answer in God's Word for you. Speaking God's Word over your life has the power to deliver you from bad situations, heal your body of sickness, renew your mind in the truth and transform your life for the better. Jesus knew this. When tempted in the garden by satan, He spoke forth God's Word..."It is written" (see Matthew 4:4, 7, 10). Jesus said: *"If you continue in My word, you really are My disciples. You will know the truth, and the truth will set you free."*

All prayer must be directed to the Father or to the Son. Notice I didn't say to Mary, John or any other prophet or saint. Our mind and heart must be directed to the Father, asking in Jesus' Name, or to Jesus, Himself, asking in His Name. And when we go to Him, we must know that He is all powerful and all knowing. He already knows what we are in need of (Matthew 6:8). He knows every hair on our head. Therefore, we do not go to Him hoping to change His mind or hoping He will open His eyes and see what is going on in our lives or to inform Him of our needs. When we go to God in prayer, we go to bring ourselves in alignment with His heart and His Will. His Will is good and perfect. Many times we ask for what we want, but if we ask according to His Will, He will grant our requests (1 John 5:14, 15).

We must go to Him, however, with unwavering faith. We must believe in our heart that God is listening and He is willing and able to grant your requests. Reject all doubt and receive it by faith. Now that is praying effectively!

THE PROVISION

RECEIVE THE PROMISES

The promises simply speak of the provision God makes for us when we are obedient to His Word. It is important that you know the promises in God's Word. As you pray, keep the following promises in mind and begin to search the Bible for other promises that pertain to your situation. They are not hard to find. There are over 3000 promises to choose from.

"This is the confidence we have in approaching God: that if we ask anything according to his will, he hears us. 15 And if we know that he hears us—whatever we ask—we know that we have what we asked of him." 1 John 5:14-15 NIV

I'm ready to perform my Word- Jeremiah 1:12

Whatever things you ask in prayer, believing, you will receive- Matthew 21:22

John 14:14-*If you ask anything in my name, I will do it.*

Be anxious for nothing- Philippians 4:6

"Commit your ways to the Lord, trust Him and He will bring it to pass."- Psalm 37:5

Isaiah 65:24 says, "It shall come to pass that before they call, I will answer; and while they are still speaking, I will hear."

Prayer demonstrates our faith in God that He will do just as He promised in His word. "My Word will not return unto me void, but shall accomplish"- Isaiah 55:11. Therefore, it is not enough to just know the promises—we must also expect to receive the manifestation of the promise.

Take a look at Mark 6:4-5. Jesus was in His hometown. Now because of the people's unbelief, Mark tells us that Jesus "could not do many mighty works or miracles there." Unbelief excluded the people of Nazareth from the dynamic disclosure of God's grace that others had experienced. This account does not indicate that Jesus lacked he power or ability to perform miracles under any circumstances, but that His hands were tied. Why? Because I believe that faith and expectation were the usual condition of His miracles.

Here are some Biblical accounts of those who through expectation received the promise:

>Matthew 8:13 - Then Jesus said to the centurion, "Go your way; and as you have believed, so let it be done for you." And his servant was healed that same hour.

>Matthew 9:2 - Then behold, they brought to Him a paralytic lying on a bed. When Jesus saw their faith, He said to the paralytic, "Son, be of good cheer; your sins are forgiven you."

Matthew 9:22 - But Jesus turned around, and when He saw her He said, "Be of good cheer, daughter; your faith has made you well." And the woman was made well from that hour.

Matthew 9:28, 29 - And when He had come into the house, the blind men came to Him. And Jesus said to them, "Do you believe that I am able to do this?" They said to Him, "Yes, Lord." Then He touched their eyes, saying, "According to your faith let it be to you."

Matthew 15:28 - Then Jesus answered and said to her, "O woman, great is your faith! Let it be to you as you desire." And her daughter was healed from that very hour.

It is important to remember that God manifests His promises in our lives for a greater purpose. It's not about us, although we receive the residue, but it's about declaring His Glory, His Sovereignty, Spreading the Gospel through our testimonies...

THE PLACE AND TIME

"I have so much to do that I shall have to spend the first three hours in prayer." –Martin Luther

A TIME AND A PLACE FOR PRAYER

"Moses went to a mountaintop to hear God. Jesus fled to the desert. But for many Christians, their most regular place for praying is whatever pew they sit in on Sundays. Work, children, chores and other duties make stopping for prayer seem a luxury. "We forget to intentionally make space for prayer," but that's not the way it's supposed to be. Souls, like vines, tend to grow wild and weak when untended." SUSAN HOGAN

We tend to have too many distractions in our lives. We must get to a place where we not only spend time alone with the Lord each day, but we also find a special place which is set aside for that purpose in our home, a quiet place. You may be thinking, "There is no place in my home that I can go and be alone with God." I say when you're desperate enough to be alone with someone, you find a place. Think back to when you wanted to be alone with the special someone. You found a place and a time. Don't short change God. My place has changed several times over the years. It has been in my closet, in my kitchen in the middle of the night, when everyone is asleep or in my truck, parked on a side street. Get creative.

> God's power is displayed in those who prioritize prayer.

God's power is displayed in those who prioritize prayer. The Word tells us in Matthew 6:33, if we seek first the Kingdom of God and His righteous, all these things will be added unto us. So if we set aside a place designated to eat and sleep, we should also set aside a place to pray. Where do you go to pray? Have you set aside a special place? How bad do you want to experience the power of God?

Martin Luther understood that he had so much work to do for God that he could never get it done unless he prayed three hours a day! Have you set aside a time? I set my cell phone alarm for certain times throughout my day. These are strategic prayers that I will discuss in detail in my next book, *"Sleeping with the Enemy"*. I also talk to God and offer praises to Him constantly as I go along my day. I just love talking to God. He is the only One I can talk to about any and everything. Scripture says that we should pray without ceasing. Don't stop. Pray every day. Don't wait for a S.O.S. or a crisis to occur before you set aside a time to pray. Pray throughout your day. We must pray even if our lives seem to be going well. "Soldiers are not trained during wartime; they are trained for combat during peacetime." (Goodman, 2004). We must strive for a 24-7 relationship with God.

THE POSTURE

POSITIONING MYSELF-PHYSICALLY

For many years, I, along with many others, believed that all prayers should be offered on our knees. However, in scripture, we can see people praying in various positions.

Read & Meditate:

- Standing before the Lord: 1 Kings 8:22; Genesis 24:12
- Lifting the hands: 1 Timothy 2:8
- Sitting: 2 Samuel 7:8; Judges 20:26
- Lying down in bed: Psalm 4:4; Psalm 63:3
- Kneeling: Daniel 6:10; Acts 7:60; Acts 9:40; 2 Chronicles 6:13; Ezra 9:5; Psalm 95:6
- Looking upward: John 17:1
- Bowing down: Exodus 4:31; Exodus 12:27; Exodus 34:8
- Prostrate (laying flat): 1 Kings 1:47; Mark 14:35; 2 Samuel 14:4
- Placing the head between the knees: 1 Kings 18:42
- Pounding on the breast : Luke 18:13
- Facing the temple: Daniel 6:10

Which posture is correct? Here's my take on the subject. The Bible exhorts us to pray without ceasing. That means, at home-pray; at the mall-pray; at work-pray; in the car-pray. There are many places and times throughout our day that we pray.

Therefore, no one position can accommodate us. Of course, we probably wouldn't drop to our knees in the middle of the mall and pray (you could if you were bold enough). It is unlikely that you would lay prostrate while driving your car. You get my drift? Your position would differ depending upon the situation, time, and place. The only wrong position is one that is uncomfortable and distracting you from communicating with God. Sometimes sitting or laying in bed causes me to fall asleep in the middle of my prayers. When I feel my eyes getting heavy, I stand up or walk around.

"The greatest tragedy of life is not unanswered prayer, but unoffered prayer." –F.B. Meyer

POSITIONING MYSELF-SPIRITUALLY

More importantly than the postures listed above is the posture of your heart. When your heart is closed to prayer, God is not obligated to work through you. I call this the closed posture. It can be best seen in most churches on Sunday morning. You know when the pastor asks everyone to stand and pray, but only half the congregation actually stands. I am not talking about those who cannot physically stand. I am talking about those who have full activity of their limbs. These Christians refuse to pray. Some even seem to be agitated when asked just to stand and agree with the prayer that is going forth. Their arms are folded, hands are in their pockets, and they seem to be searching for something in their purses. All of these gestures and attitudes symbolize a closed posture. Sadly, court judges get more respect than the Creator of all, God. When the bailiff announces, "All rise!" The entire courtroom stands. God deserves much more respect and honor than a courtroom judge. Don't you think?

There are many reasons why people's hearts are closed to prayer. Let's discuss a few that are not commonly dealt with.

They don't want anything.-Shocked? Yes, there are people who don't want anything. There are many who are satisfied with their lives, the way it is. Therefore, they never ask God for anything greater and they play it safe to avoid any ruffling of the waters. Sadly, these people never experience greater than where they are. We understand that God wants to elevate to higher heights. He wants to take us from glory to glory, but if we close Him out we will never experience His full power.

They are afraid God will respond. When I was living a life of sin—living in fornication and "shacking up," I refused to pray because I knew if I began to pray, God would begin dealing with me about clearing the mess out of my life. At the time, I thought I was not ready for that. I wanted to satisfy my flesh and continue in sin. This may sound crazy to some of you "super spiritual" people, but it was true for me and is still true for many others. God not only knows what is best for us, He has a better way. Pray and surrender!

<u>They have had previous prayers go unanswered</u>. This will be discussed in the next chapter.

<u>They don't truly believe that God can make a difference.</u> The more and more I interact with Christians, I find that most Christians do not truly believe much of what they claim to believe. They are quick to tell others how to live, how to pray, to trust God and to read the Bible, but their own behavior betrays them again and again. They rarely pray. They make decisions without consulting God. And they are determined to make their own blessings.

<u>They let things take priority over prayer.</u> The affairs and concerns of life have overshadowed most people's prayer life. Matthew 6:33 tells us that when we "Seek first His kingdom and His righteousness," and these all these things will be added to us. Some things we are petitioning God for can be ours automatically if we just seek Him first. Even pastors and others of us in ministry let things sneak in to rob us from spending quality time with God in prayer – sermon preparation, church administration, counseling, etc. Yes, these things are often

spiritual in nature, but nothing should take priority over our time with the God.

If you fit any of those categories, repent now (turn away from that way of thinking or doing things) and ask God for forgiveness. In the end, remember, it is not the body's posture, but the heart that counts when we pray. Open your heart!

THE PROBLEM

"The reason why we obtain no more in prayer is because we expect no more. God usually answers us according to our own hearts." –Richard Alleine

NOT SEEING RESULTS

Houston, there is a problem. You've sought out scriptures. You've prayed fervently. You've followed all the guidelines in this book. Yet you still have not seen your prayers manifest. Below are a few reasons your prayers are not being answered.

SIN: *Psalm 66:18 "If I regard iniquity in my heart, the Lord will not hear me."*
Before we go any further, let me say that when it comes to consistent manifestation of prayers, *HOLY LIVING* is a non-negotiable! Let's look at some scriptures that I feel speak for themselves.

"They cry out, but He [God] does not answer because of the
arrogance of evil men. *Surely God will not listen to a phony [empty] prayer [cry], nor will the Almighty regard it."*
- Job 35:12-13

"Quit your worship charades. I can't stand your trivial religious games: Monthly conferences, weekly Sabbaths, special meetings—meetings, meetings, meetings—I can't stand one more! Meetings for this, meetings for that. I hate them! You've worn me out! I'm sick of your religion, religion, religion, while you go right on

45

sinning. When you put on your next prayer-performance, I'll be looking the other way. No matter how long or loud or often you pray, I'll not be listening. And do you know why? Because you've been tearing people to pieces, and your hands are bloody. Go home and wash up. Clean up your act. Sweep your lives clean of your evildoings so I don't have to look at them any longer. Say no to wrong. Learn to do good. Work for justice. Help the down-and-out. Stand up for the homeless. Go to bat for the defenseless. "Come. Sit down. Let's argue this out." This is God's Message: "If your sins are blood-red, they'll be snow-white. If they're red like crimson, they'll be like wool. If you'll willingly obey, you'll feast like kings. But if you're willful and stubborn, you'll die like dogs." That's right. God says so.-Isaiah 1:14-20 Message. WOW! No need to elaborate. I believe Isaiah dropped the mic on that one. Completely turn away from sin and watch God answer your prayers.

WRONG MOTIVES: *James 4:2-4 is addressed to believers:* *"You lust and do not have [what you want], so you commit murder. Also, you are jealous and cannot obtain, so you fight and quarrel. You do not have, because you do not ask. You ask [in prayer] and do not receive, because **you ask with wrong motives**, so that you may spend it* *on pleasures or lusts. You adulteresses, do you not know that friendship with the world is hostility toward God? Therefore whoever wishes to be a friend of the world makes himself an enemy of God. "* It is important to note that your requests may be in line with the Word of God, but your desire behind it can be wrong and result in an unanswered prayer. The example I like to use is, I Corinthians 14:1, reads, "Pursue love, and desire spiritual gifts, but especially that you may prophesy." A person can petition God to prophesy and as we see in the scripture, that is completely biblical, but if his desire to prophesy is to impress or manipulate others, this person is a prime candidate for an unanswered prayer.

YOU NEED TO DO MORE: *"I've have cleared my life of sin. My motives are right, but still NO ANSWER! HELP!"* Don't panic. I feel your spirit. The disciples experienced the same thing. They were confronted by a man who brought his child to be healed of demons. The child was demon possessed. The disciples had graduated from the school of prayer. They received their Masters in demon casting. In fact, they had the greatest professor that has ever walked the earth. But when they attempted to cast the demons out of this child, nothing worked. What went wrong? What could have happened? Jesus simply let them know that there are some things that can only be accomplished through fasting and praying.

THE PRIVILEGE

"If the only prayer you ever say in your entire life is thank you, it will be enough." –Meister Eckhart

Praise

"And when they had laid many stripes upon them, they cast them into prison, charging the jailor to keep them safely: Who, having received such a charge, thrust them into the inner prison, and made their feet fast in the stocks. And at midnight Paul and Silas prayed, and sang praises unto God: and the prisoners heard them. And suddenly there was a great earthquake, so that the foundations of the prison were shaken: and immediately all the doors were opened, and every one's bands were loosed" Acts 16:23-26.

According to the standards of that day, prisons were dark, damp, and resembled a dungeon. Yet, in spite of the throbbing pain in their bodies and the disheartening atmosphere, at midnight Paul and Silas were heard praying and singing praises to God. What a powerful combination! Many people do not understand that praise is a vehicle of faith that not only brings us into the presence and power of God, but is one of the most powerful weapons against the enemy. What a privilege it is to be in the presence of God and receive power to overcome the enemy! The Bible tells us that praise releases angels to go forth on our behalf and to perform the Word for our lives. Praise is not something we should just do on Sunday mornings. Praise, just like prayer, should be a part of a Believer's lifestyle. We should praise Him in our homes, in our cars, on our jobs, in

> Our praises releases angels to go forth and minister on our behalf.

every situation. Paul and Silas knew the secret of how to lift their hearts above their troubles and enter into God's presence and power.

I begin all my prayers praising and worshipping God. Praise simply means "to commend, to applaud or magnify." Giving Him reverence in all things. God inhabits the praises of His people so go ahead and lift your hands (Psalms 134:2), declare thanks (Heb. 13:15), shout for joy, clap your hands (Psalms 47:1), stomp your feet, do a dance, and sing a song (Psalm 150:4) and allow Him to inhabit your heart. I continue to praise God until I feel His inhabitation, His presence. Then I am empowered to move forth in prayer.

Below I included scriptures to meditate on. Allow them to get into your spirit and let your praise manifest from your heart. My spiritual mother says we should "think and thank." Think about His goodness, what He has done for us, and what He has brought us through. Then thank Him. Pour out your heart to Him in thanksgiving. It takes your eyes off the problem and allows you to see that God is the one that is in control.

Read & Meditate: Psalm 22:3
"Enter into his gates with thanksgiving, and into his courts with praise: be thankful unto him, and bless his name" (Psalms 100:4).

Heavenly Father, I bow in worship and praise before You. I surrender myself completely and unreservedly in every area of my life to You. My whole being follows hard after You and clings closely to You. What can I withhold from You? The heavens are Yours. The earth is Yours. The world and all that is in it is Yours. You formed it. Psalm 63:8; Psalm 89:11. God I thank and praise You for all that I have and all that I am.

O' God, You are the Mighty One. You speak and call the earth from the rising of the sun to its setting. Your loving kindness is better than life itself. Your right hand upholds me. How awesome and fearfully glorious are Your works! Who can compare to You? Psalm 50:1; Psalm 63:3; Psalm 66:3

Lord, I recognize that You are worthy to receive all glory and honor and praise. You have proven Your power by resurrecting Jesus Christ from the dead. Thank you Father, that through Jesus, I can claim in every way, victory over all satanic forces in my life. I am an overcomer because He who is in me is greater than he that is in the world. From this day forth, I will stand and see this great thing which You are doing before my eyes. 1 John 4:4; 1 Samuel 12:16

Rejoice in the Lord always. Again I say Rejoice! Let my prayers be set before You as incense, the lifting of my hands as the evening sacrifice. Philippians 4:4; Psalm 141:2

I bless You, Lord O' my soul and with all that is within me, I will bless Your Holy Name. Yours O' Lord is the greatness and the power and the glory and the victory and the majesty for all that is in the heavens and the earth is Yours. Yours is the kingdom O' Lord and Yours it is to be exalted as Head over all. Both riches and honor come from You and You reign over all. In Your hands is power and might; in Your hands is to make great and to give strength to all. Psalm 103; 1 Chronicles 29:11, 12

"You are worthy, O' Lord, to receive glory and honor and power; for You created all things, And by Your will they exist and were created." (Revelation 4:11).

You set the universe into motion and made the earth in wisdom and beauty, and You are the source of life. From everlasting to everlasting You alone are God the All Sufficient One!

NAMES OF GOD

God's names are dynamic and they are full of power. In fact, they along with the Name and the Blood of Jesus are some of our most powerful weapons against satan. In fact, no power of darkness can stand against these weapons.

God reveals great truths about Himself that can be found only in His names. Pray to God and ask Him to give you insight into each of His names. Ask Him to teach you about His character and attributes.

"O Magnify the Lord with me, and let us exalt His name together." Psalms 34:3

"I will bow down toward Your holy temple and will praise Your Name for Your love and Your faithfulness, for You have exalted above all things Your Name and Your Word." Psalms 138:2

Study the following list of God's Names. Ask God to show you how to apply them in your prayer life. Use God's Names to cry out to Him in every need. Scriptures tells us.

"Our help is in the Name of the Lord, Who made heaven and earth." Psalms 124:8.

Adonai-Jehovah Genesis 12:2, 8
Advocate 1 John 2:1
All and All Colossians 3:11
Anchor Hebrews 6:19
Angel of His Presence Isaiah 63:9
Apostle and High Priest Hebrews 3:1
Arm of the Lord Isaiah 51:9
Author of our Faith Hebrews 12:2
Balm of Gilead Jeremiah 8:22
Banner for the Nations Isaiah 11:12

Blessed and Only Potentate 1 Timothy 6:15
Bright and Morning Star Revelations 22:16
Captain of Our Salvation Hebrews 2:10
Captain of the Host of the Lord Joshua 5:14
Chief Cornerstone 1 Peter 2:6
Chief Shepherd 1 Peter 5:4
Christ the Power of God 1 Corinthians 1:24
Consuming Fire Hebrews 12:29
Cover from the Tempest Isaiah 32:2
Deliverer Romans 11:26
Emmanuel – God With Us Matthew 1:23
Faithful and True Revelation 19:11
Father of Mercies 2 Corinthians 1:3
Flame Isaiah 10:17
Fountain of Living Waters Jeremiah 17:13-14
Friend who sticks closer than a brother Proverbs 18:24
Glorious Lord Isaiah 33:21
God of All Comfort 2 Corinthians 1:3
God of All Grace 1 Peter 5:10
God of Hope Romans 15:13
God of Peace Romans 15:33
God of My Life Psalms 42:8
God of Truth Deuteronomy 32:4
God the Judge of All Hebrews 12:23
Governor Matthew 2:6
Great High Priest Hebrews 4:14
Great King Over All the Earth Psalms 47:2
Great King above all gods Psalms 95:3
Great Light Isaiah 9:2
Great Shepherd of the Sheep Hebrews 13:20
Head of Every Man 1 Corinthians 11:3
Head Over All Things Ephesians 1:22
Health of My Countenance Psalms 42:11
He Who Shall Have Dominion Numbers 24:19
Hiding Place from the Wind Isaiah 32:2
High and Lofty One Isaiah 57:15
Holy and Awesome Psalms 111:9
Holy One of God Luke 4:34
Hope of Glory Colossians 1:27

I AM John 8:58
Jehovah-Elyon – The Lord Most High Psalms 7:17
Jehovah-Jireh – The Lord Will Provide Genesis 22:8
Jehovah-Mekaddishkem –The Lord Our Sanctifier
Leviticus 20:8
Jehovah-Nissi – The Lord My Banner Exodus 17:15
Jehovah-Rohi – The Lord My Shepherd Psalms 23:1
Jehovah-Rapha – The Lord My Healer Exodus 15:26
Jehovah-Sabaoth – The Lord of Hosts 1 Samuel 1:3
Jehovah-Shalom – The Lord of Our Peace Judges 6:24
Jehovah-Shammah – The Lord Is There Ezekiel 48:35
Jehovah-Tsidkenu – The Lord Our Righteousness Jeremiah 23:6
Jesus Christ the Righteous 1 John 2:1
Judge of the Living and the Dead Acts 10:42
King in His Beauty Isaiah 33:17
King of Kings Revelation 17:14
King Over All the Earth Zechariah 14:9
Lamb in the Midst of the Throne Revelation 7:17
Lamb of God John 1:29
Lamb Slain Revelation 5:12
Lamb without Blemish 1 Peter 1:19
Life Giving Spirit 1 Corinthians 15:45
Light of the World John 8:12
Lion of the Tribe of Judah Revelation 5:5
Lord Romans 10:13
Lord and Savior Jesus Christ 2 Peter 3:18
Lord of Both the Dead and Living Romans 14:9
Lord God Almighty Revelation 4:8
Lord God of Truth Psalms 31:5
Lord God Omnipotent Revelation 19:6
Lord Jesus Christ of Nazareth Luke 4:34
Lord Mighty in Battle Psalms 24:8
Lord Most High Psalms 47:2
Lord of All Acts 10:36
Lord of All the Earth Zechariah 6:5
Lord Jehovah Psalms 83:18, Isaiah 26:4
Lord of Hosts Psalms 24:10
Lord of lords Revelation 17:14
Lord Our Maker Psalms 95:6

Lord Our Righteousness Jeremiah 23:6
Lord Over All Romans 10:12
Lord Strong and Mighty Psalms 24:8
Lord Your Redeemer Isaiah 43:14
Love 1 John 4:8
Man of War Exodus 15:3
Mediator 1 Timothy 2:5
Mediator of a Better Covenant Hebrews 8:6
Mediator of the New Covenant Hebrews 12:24
Messiah John 4:25
Mighty God Isaiah 9:6
Mighty One Psalms 45:3
Mighty One of Israel Isaiah 30:29
Most High – Highest Psalms 18:13
Most Holy Daniel 9:24
My Fortress Psalms 144:2
My Help Psalms 115:11
My Helper Hebrews 13:6
My High Tower Psalms 144:2
My Hope Psalms 71:5
My Lord and My God John 20:28
My Strength and My Power 2 Samuel 22:33
My Rock of Refuge Psalms 31:2
My Salvation Psalms 38:22
My Shield 2 Samuel 22:3, Psalms 144:21
My Song Isaiah 12:2
My Support – My Stay Psalms 18:18
Our Great God 2 Chronicles 20:12
Our Passover 1 Corinthians 5:7
Our Peace Ephesians 2:14
Overcoming Lamb Revelation 17:14
Priest Forever Hebrews 5:6
Prince of Life Acts 3:15
Prince of Peace Isaiah 9:6
Redeemer Isaiah 59:20
Refiner and Purifier Malachi 3:3
Refuge from the Storm Isaiah 25:4
Resting Place Jeremiah 50:6
Restorer Psalms 23:3

Rewarder Hebrews 11:6
Rock Deuteronomy 32:4
Rock That Is Higher Than I Psalms 61:2
Rod of Your Strength Psalms 110:2
Ruler Micah 5:2
Ruler Over The Kings Of The Earth Revelation 1:5
Sanctuary Isaiah 8:14
Shadow of a Great Rock in a Weary Land Isaiah 32:2
Shepherd Genesis 49:24
Shepherd of Israel Psalms 80:1
Shelter of His People Psalms 91:1
Shield Psalms 3:3, Psalms 115:11
Shield of Your Help Deuteronomy 33:29
Shiloh (Peacemaker) Genesis 49:10
Son of God John 1:34
Son of the Highest Luke 1:32
Son of the Most High God Mark 5:7
Spirit of Justice Isaiah 28:5-6
Strength of My Life Psalms 27:1
Strength to the Needy Isaiah 25:4
Strong Lord Psalms 89:8
Strong Tower Psalms 61:3
Stronghold Nahum 1:7
Sun and Shield Psalms 84:11
Sure Foundation Isaiah 28:16
Surety Hebrews 7:22
Sword of Your Excellency Deuteronomy 33:29
Testator Hebrews 9:16
That Eternal Life 1 John 1:2
That Spiritual Rock 1 Corinthians 10:4
The Alpha and the Omega Revelations 22:13
The Beginning and the End Revelations 22:13
The Root and the Offspring of David Revelations 22:16
The Way, the Truth, the Life John 14:6
Trap and a Snare Isaiah 8:14
Tried Stone Isaiah 28:16
True Bread of Heaven John 6:32
True Light John 1:9
Tower of Salvation 2 Samuel 22:51

True God 1 John 5:20
Understanding Proverbs 8:14
Upholder of All Things Hebrews 1:3
Vine John 15:5
Wisdom Proverbs 8:12
Wonderful Isaiah 9:6
Wisdom of God 1 Corinthians 1:24
Witness to the People Isaiah 55:4
Word John 1:1
Word of God Revelation 19:13
Word of Life 1 John 1:1
Worthy Lamb Revelation 5:12
Your Confidence Proverbs 3:26
Your Everlasting Light Isaiah 60:20
Your Exceeding Great Reward Genesis 15:1
Your Holy One Acts 2:27
Your Keeper Psalms 121:5
Your King Zechariah 9:9
Your Maker Isaiah 54:5
Your Shade Psalms 121:5
Your Shield Genesis 15:1

THE PRAYERS

SIN

Darkness cannot dwell with light. Sin separates us from God; He is perfect and cannot tolerate the presence of sin. Sin is anything that goes against God and His operation in our life. Sin should be confessed, repented and committed to prayer. Failing to do so allows satan an open door into your life.

Read & Meditate: 1 John 1:8-10; Romans 6:23; Daniel 9:4-19; Psalm 32:5-7

CONFESS SIN AND RECEIVE THE SON

I have sinned and done wrong. I have rebelled against You and scorned Your commands and regulations. Father, I know that my sins have caused me to remove myself from Your protection and covering. I am truly sorry, and now I want to turn away from my past and present sinful life toward You. I never want to experience life without You. For You are my hiding place; You protect me from trouble. Please forgive me, and help me avoid sinning again. I believe that Your Son, Jesus Christ died for my sins, was resurrected from the dead, is alive, and hears my prayer. I invite Jesus to become the Lord of my life, to rule and reign in my heart from this day forward. Please send Your Holy Spirit to help me obey You, and to do Your will for the rest of my life. In Jesus' name I pray, Amen.

SECRET SINS

Lord I have repented for all of my surface level sins, but God, this is about the secret sins which I have managed, I think, to conceal from others but which are an open book to You. Father, You see the sly dishonesty, the creeping pride, the selfish preoccupation, the lustful thoughts, the abusive actions, the crooked business dealings, the tight-fisted stinginess and the fear of facing consequences I deserve. Remove everything and every person in my life the devil has assigned to me to keep me from you. Remove from me any double mindedness, hindrances, obstacles, invisible walls, Lord anything in my life or on the throne of my life that does not belong. Cleanse me thoroughly of all demonic residues I have come into contact with in my dealings. If there is any area or anything in my life that is not totally submitted to the mind of Christ, I give you permission and ask You to cause these things to come down to the obedience of Christ. In the Mighty name of Jesus...My Savior...My Deliverer...My Redeemer.

CLEANSING

Even if you believe you don't need it or that you haven't done anything, remember, no one walked this earth perfectly but Jesus.

"If anyone sins and does what is forbidden in any of the Lord's commands, even though they do not know it they are guilty and will be held responsible."-Leviticus 5:17 NIV.

You said if I confess my sins You are faithful and just to forgive me of my sins and cleanse me from ALL unrighteousness. So Lord Jesus Christ I come to You now, I receive my forgiveness and cleansing from all unrighteousness: spot, wrinkle and blemish free, totally blameless, from the top of my head to the soles of my feet. You said if I confess my sins You are faithful and just to forgive me of my sins and cleanse me from ALL unrighteousness. So Lord Jesus Christ I come to You now, I receive my forgiveness and cleansing from all unrighteousness: spot, wrinkle and blemish free, totally blameless, from the top of my head to the soles of my feet, at the dendritic and quantum level, in Jesus Christ's Holy name. I empty myself and, as an empty vessel, receive you Holy Spirit for the work you would have me do this day for your glory. Holy Spirit I ask You to pray to my Lord in Heaven to remove from me any hindrances, any obstacles, double mindedness, and duplicity, anything in my life or on the throne of my life that does not belong. I come to you in full submission to your will in my life. In Your name, I pray. Lord, if there is anything or area in my life that is not totally submitted to the mind of Christ, I give You permission and ask You to cause these areas and/or things to come down now to the obedience of the mind of Christ within me, in Jesus Christ's Holy name.

THE BLOOD OF JESUS

The Blood of Jesus is so powerful that it saved mankind from eternal damnation. The Blood not only saves but it protects, forgives, and delivers us from sin and the power of darkness.

Read & Meditate: Exodus 12:22; Leviticus 17:11; 1 Peter 1:18, 19; Colossians 1:13, 14; 1 John 1:7; Hebrews 9:12; Hebrews 9:24-26; Luke 22:20; Romans 3:25; Acts 20:28; Revelations 12:11; Ephesians 2:13-14; Ephesians 1:7; Hebrews 10:19; Hebrews 2:14

O' THE BLOOD

O' The Blood! Thank You Father for the Blood! I thank You that I don't have to plead the Blood because to plead means to beg. I have the authority and power available by the death and resurrection of Jesus to apply the Blood and proclaim the victory that is mine through the Blood. It is my priesthood right. Therefore, I proclaim the victory of the blood of Jesus! I am blood-washed, blood-bought, blood-justified, blood-sanctified, blood- safe, blood-ransomed. Father, You said in Exodus12:13-14, that the blood shall be a sign of protection and covering throughout the generations. By faith, I sprinkle the Blood of Jesus on my doorposts; I draw the Bloodline of Jesus around family, myself and all that we possess in Jesus name. Thank you, Father for the precious Blood of the Lord Jesus Christ. O' The Blood!

ANXIETY & WORRY

We all know what it feels like to be anxious. Most of us experience anxiety when we're faced with stressful situations or traumatic events. Busy schedules, intensified by traffic jams, money problems, and relational difficulties also keep many people in chronic states of stress. But if anxiety is disrupting your normal everyday life and causes overwhelming fear, worry, and stress, it must be dealt with. Anxiety should be committed to prayer. Philippians 4:6-7 says: "Do not be anxious about anything, but in everything, by prayer and petition, with thanksgiving, present your requests to God. And the peace of God, which transcends all understanding, will guard your hearts and your minds in Christ Jesus".

Read & Meditate: 1 John 4:8; I Peter 5:6-7; Luke 12:22-26; NIV, Isaiah 41:10; Psalm 23:4; Psalm 34:4; Psalm 55:22 NASB; Psalm 138:8; Psalm 18:1-3 NKJV; Matthew 11:28 NIV; Ephesians 2:14-17; Ephesians 6:10-11

STRESSED OUT

I come to You because I feel weary and heavily burdened seeking rest. I cast ALL my burdens upon You, Lord—all those things and people that worry me, stress me, or cause me to be angry and confused. I believe that You will sustain me and never allow me to be shaken. I trust that You will perfect those things which concern me. I love You. You are my strength, my rock, my fortress, my deliverer, my shield, my stronghold…You are worthy to be praised above all. You never sleep nor slumber therefore, I can go to sleep and have peace knowing that You have it all under control. I realize that peace is not the absence of outer turmoil, trial, tribulation, but the presence of inner rest in Christ Jesus.

HELP! I'M DROWNING!

Lord, Help me. Everywhere I turn trouble is all around me. I am pressed: troubled on every hand. When I feel like I've won one battle, another one ensues. At times I feel like I am drowning and gasping for breath. I'm tempted to throw in the towel. Oh but I remember Your Word that says when the enemy comes in like a flood, Your Holy Spirit will lift up a standard against him. I thank You God that You are my spiritual lifeguard and that You have already defeated and delivered me from the hand of the evil one. Therefore, I stand strong in You and in the power of Your might.

PRAYER FOR SLEEP

I come against all demons of the night, nightmares, bad dreams, torment, sleeplessness, torture. I command these demons to loose me and come out of me, and I ask that you protect my mind while I sleep. I sprinkle the Blood Jesus over the gates of my home and the doorpost of my bedroom, in JESUS' name.

JEALOUSY & ENVY

Jealousy is a sign of immaturity and carnality. Jealousy is resenting the fact that God has allowed others to have something, do something, or be something that you wish you had, could do, or were. It says to God that we do not trust His judgment for it is He who gives all good things. Whether it is a conscious word or a thought in the back-of-your-mind, jealousy is something we all struggle with daily. Sometimes those little thoughts that creep into our minds don't sound like jealousy... but are they? The effects of jealousy and envy can be disastrous to your spiritual well-being.

Read & Meditate: Proverbs 14:30; Galatians 5:26; James 3:16; I Peter 2:1; Proverbs 23:17; Psalm 37:1-2; Psalm 49:16-17; 1 Corinthians 12:18; 1 Corinthians 13:4; Songs of Solomon 8:6; Ephesians 4:11

JEALOUSY: I SUPPLIETH

Lord, help me to understand that it is You who has set me in the body, as You please. And because of that, when I feel jealous and envious of someone else's blessings, gifts, or calling, I am actually showing anger towards You—the one who created, gifted, called and blessed me. I repent and ask that You forgive me. Help me to walk in love with my brothers and sisters in Christ because love is not envious and jealous is as strong as death. Help me to see that my role, my calling is just as important in the kingdom as someone else's. Help me to clearly see what role I play—how I supplieth the Body of Christ. Help me to focus on my assignment. In the name of Jesus, I renounce all envy, jealousy, and covetousness that have taken a hold of me.

SICKNESS

God has commissioned us to do great exploits for the Kingdom. The reality is that if our bodies and minds are riddled with sickness, we limit what God can do through us. Many Christians live defeated lives battling sickness and disease while the truth is Jesus Christ not only healed people when on the earth, but He still heals people today! Healing is our birthright.

Read & Meditate: Ex. 15:26, Ex. 23:25-26, Deut 7:15, Ps 91:9-10, Ps 103:1-5, Ps 107:19-20, Prov. 4:20-23, Isa 41:10, Isa 53:4-5, Isa 55:9-11, Isa 58:6-11, Jer. 30:17, Mal. 3:6, Mal. 4:2-3, Matt 7:7-11, Matt 8:16-17, Matt 9:35, Matt 15:30-31, Mark 11:22-24, Mark 16:17-18, Luke 4:17-19, Luke 9:1-2, Luke 10:8-9, Luke 13:16, Acts 4:29-30, Acts 5:15-16, Acts 10:38, Gal 3:13, James 5:13-16, 1 John 5:14-15, 3 John 2, Romans 12:1, Psalm 116:8-9

HEALING

(Start by giving God praise)

Father, in the Name of Jesus, I confess Your Word concerning my healing. I am the Body of Christ. Because my body is the house of God, sickness and disease has no place in me. Lord, separate me completely from all the sins of my father, mother and forefathers by the precious blood of Jesus. Remove in the mighty name of Jesus any curses and help me to see the deceptions of the enemy that have crept in unknowingly and caused me to walk disobediently- unaware that a curse was placed upon and in my lineage. Now, with great boldness and confidence I say on the authority of the written word that I am redeemed from the curse of sickness and I refuse to tolerate its symptoms. Satan, I loose your grips in the name of Jesus. You foul spirit of infirmity get out of my body! Come out in the Name of Jesus of Nazareth! Take your pain, sickness, and disease with you! Go to the pits of hell and stay there! I declare a death sentence on sickness. Sickness dry up and come out of my body in the Name of Jesus! I declare and decree and establish healing in my body from the top of my head to the soul of my feet. I am healthy and strong—physically, emotionally, and spiritually—because I am one with God. I am a child of the King, the Most High; therefore, my position at the table of the Lord is already set. The enemy is defeated because I dwell in the secret place of the Most High God. You came with healing in Your wings and You paid the price for my peace and wholeness. By faith I receive God's complete healing given to me by the stripes that wounded Jesus. I am Your property. I am healed!

FORGIVENESS FOR NOT TAKING CARE OF GOD'S TEMPLE

Father, I know that my body is a temple for You to dwell and do Your good works. I have not taken care of this body You've given me the way I should. I come to You today asking for Your forgiveness. I give no praise to the devil because I know that because of my poor choices I brought sickness over myself. But even in this, I will acknowledge You, I will bless You and I will praise You. I thank You for another chance. For You have delivered my soul from death, my eyes from tears, and my feet from falling. I thank You that I walk in the land of the living. Now I ask that You would lead me and guide me in the way in which You desire for me to eat and take care of myself.

THANKING GOD FOR HEALING

God I thank You for restoring my health. I thank You for the example in Matthew 12:13, where you told the man to "stretch forth thine hand and he stretched it forth, and it was restored whole, like as the other." I thank You for the example in Mark 8:25, of you healing the blind man and his sight was restored and he saw clearly. I thank You that You said in Jeremiah 30:17, "For I will restore health unto thee, and I will heal thy wounds." I thank You that You are true to Your word.

MARRIAGE

Too many couples wait for signs of trouble before they invite God into their marriage. Pray and confess daily with your spouse. Practice praying for your marriage in good and bad times.

Read & Meditate: Ephesians 5:25; Mark 10:8-9; Malachi 2:16; Ephesians 5:22; Ephesians 4:32; Mark 10:9; Ephesians 5:31; Matthew 10:36; Psalm 23:3; I Peter 3:1; Romans 10:20

UNITY

Father, You are Lord over our marriage — over this union that we believe has been ordained by You. We confess Your Word over our life together. We both come into agreement and regularly seek out Your plan for us as a couple. Even though life sometimes brings trying times, we stand firm together. We will not tolerate strife or disharmony in our marriage. We declare that what you put together no man, demon or situation can put asunder. Divorce is not an option in our marriage. Our marriage will not be what the enemy wants it to be, but what God says it is in Jesus Name. We loose the Asmodeus and the Osmodeus spirits from our marriage. We bind them together and cast them into the pits of hell never to return again. We bind to ourselves love, unity, peace, and understanding. Thank You, Father, we love each other more and more each day and that our marriage grows stronger each day because it is founded on Your Word.

MARRIAGE IN TROUBLE

Lord, the enemy seeks to devour my marriage. You said that whatsoever You join together, let no man put asunder. Father, let all giants standing against peace and unity in my marriage fall down and die now in the name of Jesus. I understand that a house divided against itself cannot stand so I ask that You reunite us as one. Reveal to us exactly what's causing division in our marriage and show us how to effectively pray. Help us to see the power of unity and covenant. We repent of any sins and break all generational or bloodline curses that would defile this marriage. Restore back onto us every good and divine opportunity that we have lost to the enemy of our marriage, in the name Jesus.

ADULTERER

Father I ask you to separate (spouse name) from (name of person with whom spouse is having an affair) as far as the East is from the West. Lord, break every ungodly soul tie. Reveal what is hidden in darkness and take the blinders off of my spouse's eyes. Bring conviction upon them and take the pleasure out of their relationship right now in the name of Jesus. Cause them to repent and walk away from each other never to return again. In the name of Jesus, I break, cancel, destroy, and render null and void all spirits of lust, witchcraft, hexes, vexes, mesmerism, seduction, fornication and the spirit of Asmodeus. I command that all residues from these spirits be blown away. Lord fill every void in their heart, mind, and spirit. In the name of Jesus I bind (spouse name)'s body, soul and spirit to the will and purposes of God for his/her life. I bind (spouse name)'s mind, will and emotions to the will of God.

PRAYER FOR UNSAVED HUSBAND

Father, I come to You today lifting up my husband's soul to You. Lord Jesus Christ, I stand in the gap for (name). I ask that You will continually direct his steps and lead him in the path of righteousness for Your name sake. I pray that He will have a deep and ever-growing hunger and thirst for You and for Your Word. Father, I stand on Your Word that says if I yield to my husband and live uprightly before him, he will be persuaded to believe in You without me or anyone else saying a word. My husband submits himself to Christ, Who is the head of the man. My husband is my head and we are subject one to the other out of reverence for Christ. I call him born-again, sealed by the Holy Spirit, Spirit-filled, healed and delivered from all oppression of the enemy.

PRAYER FOR UNSAVED WIFE

Father, I come before Your throne as husband, prayer warrior, and priest of my household. Lord Jesus Christ, Your promise to me in Your Word is that my household and I will be saved. Therefore, standing on Your Holy Word, I pray that my wife's eyes would be opened, and that You would reveal Yourself in a way only my wife would be able to understand. Bring her to repentance so that she will choose to turn away from her sins and accept You into her heart. Thank You, Father that you are opening her eyes and you are turning her from darkness into your marvelous light where she will receive her rightful inheritance in Christ Jesus.

FORGIVENESS

Forgiveness is essential for life; it frees us from past wrongs and gives us hope for the future.

Read & Meditate: Proverbs 17:9; 2 Chronicles 7:14; Psalm 51:10-12; Matthew 6:14; Matthew 18:21-22; Matthew 18:35; Colossians 3:13; Mark 11:25; Matthew 5:44; Luke 6:35

I AM FREE!-FORGIVENESS
Shine the light of Your Spirit upon me and fill me with Your love. Teach me to bless those who curse me. Show me how to love my enemies and to do good to them that hate me. Father, remind me to pray for those who have despitefully used and persecuted me. Create in me a clean heart and renew a right Spirit within me. I do not want my heart to become hardened because of offense and forgiveness. God most of all I do not want anything to come between You and me. I confess today that I have been angry and bitter towards (name of person). I ask that You help me so that I may be free and able to walk in Your light. "Father, in Christ Jesus' name, I repent and lay down at Your feet all present and past forgiveness, anger, bitterness, or resentment, directed at (name of person). Help me to live in ongoing forgiveness because I choose to follow Jesus' example of forgiveness. From this moment on, satan no longer has me in

bondage and in the deadly trap of offense. I am Free! Unconditional love is in my chromosomes.

PRAY FOR THOSE WHO PERSCUTE ME: SEVEN TIMES SEVENTY

I deserve to live a life free from hatred and resentment. I treat others the way I want to be treated; therefore, I forgive those who hurt me. When I have trouble getting past an offense and treating a person with grace, I think about what Jesus has done for me on the cross. So today I pray for my haters. I speak God's blessings over their lives. I pray that You wrap them so tight in their God-given purpose that they do not have the time or the desire to persecute others.

FORGIVE THE ONE IN THE MIRROR

I refuse to dwell on discouragement because I know that every past mistake, failure, and disappointment is another step forward. Today is the day I look in the mirror and tell the person staring back at me, "I forgive you." Now, I move on into the future with new hope, a fresh perspective, and a brand new image, in Jesus' Name.

FAITH

When roadblocks and obstacles get in our way, we have to know that God is faithful to His Word.

Read & Meditate: Hebrews 10:38

I JUST GOT TO DO THIS-WALK IT OUT

I Just Got to Do This! No longer will I wait on things to come to me. I take off the spiritual blindfolds and I will go and discover those opportunities that You have set in place all around me. I Just Got to Do This! God I thank You that no matter what it looks like, I am always victorious in You. I Just Got to Do This! No giant and no mountain shall overcome me. I Just Got to Do This! The things that are impossible with man are possible for me because You dwell in me. I Just Got to Do This! I am empowered to prosper because You have blessed me with all spiritual blessings in heavenly places in Christ Jesus. I Just Got to Do This! Yes, everything will work out fine because greater is He that's in me. I Just Got to Do This! When bad things happen or trouble comes my way, I don't have to worry because You turn it around for my good. I Just Got to Do This! I don't have to go at it alone, You will never leave me nor forsake me. I Just Got to Do This! God is able to do exceedingly and abundantly above all, because He is faithful who promised! I Just Got to Believe This! I Just Got to Receive This! I Just Got to Do This!

PURITY & HOLINESS

Purity and holiness are areas that many of us struggle or have struggled with. Even those who have committed their lives to Jesus can find themselves struggling against impure thoughts and lustful feelings, partaking in sexual sins (fornication, masturbation, adultery, etc). In their quest to attain holiness and righteousness they long to be set free.

Read & Meditate: 1 Corinthians 6:19-20; 1 Thessalonians 4:3; Hebrews 4:15; James 1:12; James 4:1-3; 1 Peter 2:11; Ephesians 5:1-3, 5; Revelation 21:7-8; Galatians 5:19-21; 2 Peter 2:9

WHILE I WAIT

While I wait I will move ahead, bold and confident that You, God, are with me. While I wait I will serve and worship You in Spirit and in Truth. While I wait I will prepare myself to be who You called me to be. While I wait I will not grow weary and turn to the world. While I wait I will run this race and not be distracted by those who do not understand or support the dreams and visions you have given me. Yes Lord even while I wait.

SINGLE WOMAN'S PRAYER FOR PURITY

I keep myself Holy until marriage. I release any desperation and allow love to find me. I know God is preparing the perfect mate to be in covenant agreement with me. I walk in the Spirit;

therefore, the Holy Spirit controls my life and my desires. I always walk uprightly and the generation of the upright shall be blessed. Keep my mind occupied with Your plans and purposes; things that are holy and pure and not on the things of this world. I know it's Your will that I abstain from sexual immorality and I pray that You will keep me from seeking false intimacy through sex and sexual perversion. I cast out all spirits of loneliness that would drive me to ungodly sexual relationships in the name of Jesus. Lord, teach me to possess my body in sanctification and honor for my body is Your holy temple.

A PRAYER OF VICTORY OVER THE SPIRITS OF LUST

I come boldly before Your throne of grace and mercy to find help and strength in my time of need. Lord Your word says to watch and pray so that we will not enter into temptation, for we know that the spirit is willing, but Father my flesh is weak. Father, I know in my weakness You are made strong. Lord, I lift up all my struggles and challenges in dealing with the spirits of lust this day. I come before You today asking for deliverance. In the name of Jesus, I bind the spirits of lust, fornication, pornography, masturbation and every other spirit of lust named or unnamed and loose all you demonic spirits from your assignment of any further attacks on me and my loved ones. Spirits of lust, you no longer have control over me from this day forward, in the name of Jesus. I release the fire of God to burn out all unclean lust from my life in the name of Jesus. Father, I pray that You will cause me to think upon those things which are pure, honest, and of a good report, and I pray that You will not allow my mind to wander into idleness, but to stay upon the name of Jesus. I put on the Lord Jesus Christ and make no provision for the flesh to fulfill its lusts. I take authority over satan. I cast every lustful thought out of my head immediately, in the name of Jesus. I know the eyes are the door to the heart, and Your words says to guard my heart with all diligence. So Father, please help me to guard my heart. Father, I apply the Blood of the Lord Jesus Christ to my eyes, to cleanse them of any defilement, wickedness, or garbage I have watched that is not of You. As God's son/daughter now dedicated to remain pure and holy, I delete all pornographic pictures, visions, and dreams, lustful experiences and records in my mind, spirit and body and I commit to You, dear Lord, to living my life for you, realizing that my body is a temple which will be respected as much as I respect you. "Create in me a clean heart, and renew a steadfast spirit within me. Do no cast me away from Your presence, and please don't take Your Holy Spirit away from me.

PATIENCE & WAITING

When we pray, we often equate the lack of immediate results with God rejecting our prayers. Waiting and having patience is hard, but necessary.

Read & Meditate: Habakkuk 2:3 NIV; James 5:8; Galatians 6:9; Hebrews 6:12; Hebrews 10:35-36; Psalm 37:7

PAYDAY IS COMING

I hold on to my confidence in God because I know My Payday is coming. While I wait on the manifestation, I reflect on and rest in Your Power. You are the Proven One; the One who has shown Himself faithful even unto my ancestors. No matter what happens, whether my enemies come against me to devour my flesh, or armies arise to war against me, I will follow David's example and be absolutely confident in You. Because I know Your Word is true...My Payday is coming! All I have to do is go to sleep and wake up...go to sleep and wake up...because I am fully persuaded despite how it may look or how long it make take that my Payday is coming!

WALK IT OUT WHILE YOU WAIT

Faith without works is dead. I must continue to move, think, and act like the promise has already come to pass because I trust God while I'm waiting. I allow my waiting to build performance and perseverance. As I walk, fear, doubt, and disenchantment are left behind. As I walk, I tread over snakes (those who seek to deceive and destroy me), scorpions (those who try to sting and poison me), and all the enemy's tricks and tactics to deter me or cause me to turn back.

I'M CLOSER THAN I THINK
Father, I know that Your thoughts are not my thoughts. I know that You are able to do exceedingly and abundantly above all that I can ask or think. It feels like each time I think I'm close something happens to discourage, distract, or detour me away from my goals. God I ask that You eliminate any involvement with trivial pursuits that waste my time deterring me from the plans that You have for me. Allow me not to be distracted by those who do not understand or support the dreams and visions You have given me.

ADDICTIONS & TEMPTATIONS

When we think of addictions, drugs and alcohol often comes to mind; however, people can develop addictions to substances, behaviors or activities such as smoking, eating, sex, and even shopping. These may seem small but can quickly control our thinking and our habits. They become gods. The Bible tells us that we cannot serve two masters. Choose today who you will serve.

Read & Meditate: Galatians 5:24; Romans 6:6; Matthew 6:13; Hebrews 4:15; James 1:13-14; James 4:2; Colossians 3:2; Ephesians 5:18; I Corinthians 6:12; Galatians 5:1, 13; Lev 17:11

DRUGS & ALCOHOL

God has given me the power to transform my life. I repent of ensnaring myself and becoming a slave to drugs & alcohol and allowing evil powers to rule over me. I repent of allowing my fleshly desires and appetites to rule me. Lord, guide me with Your Holy Spirit. I repent of allowing the drug to enter and mingle with my blood. For the life...is in the blood... Please deliver me from this union with drugs. I take back the dominion that I have given the devil over my life through the use of drugs. I hand it back to you God. I am in control of my urges and desires. No person, place, or thing has any power over me. I declare that I am free!   When I am tempted to

84

_____, I acknowledge the urge, then I set it aside. Instead of feeding my addiction, I will feed my faith. My mind is back in charge. I exert control over my body's unhealthy cravings. I am breaking old habits and developing new ways of thinking. It all seems overwhelming, but I know that nothing is too hard for God. I gain the strength of every temptation I resist. I feel free, because I release myself from the yoke of leading a double life. Today, I set myself on the path to freedom by adapting a lifestyle of honesty and openness. I am committed to being free, and the only actions I take today are ones that support my success. All desire for _____ has left me. As I move forward, God help me to let go of people who drag me down and help me to recognize those who really love me and want me to be free. The Word of God says that whoever Jesus sets free is free, indeed. I decree these things over my life and call myself free, by trusting faith in Jesus this day and every day to come.

ADDICTED LOVED ONE

Father, I come to you lifting up (addicted one's name). I ask for deliverance and breakthrough in the area of (name of addiction) addiction. Wherever (addicted one's name) is now God arrest him/her now in the name of Jesus. I loose from him/her every demonic spirit of lies, manipulation, and excuses that is tormenting him/her. I bind together every loose spirit and cast them into the abyss. I bind (addicted one's name) to Your Word,

O' God. Open his/he eyes. Show (addicted one's name) the root issues that are empowering this addiction. In the name of Jesus permanently divorce (addicted one) from the spirit of... (Name the drugs they have used or the addiction) and its influence and dominion over (addicted one's name). I break all ungodly soul ties with drug dealers, enabler and co-laborers in addiction.

FOOD ADDICTION

Good food and I have been friends since I can remember. It's hard cutting off someone you love, but sometimes it's necessary. Especially if your loved one is stopping you from living the life that God has designed for you to live. One of my favorite gospel songs says, "Clap your hands and leap for joy." I have the clap down to a science, but with the extra weight it becomes a little hard to "leap for joy." If you're addicted to food, it's time to break free and receive deliverance.

FAT FREEDOM

I have nearly thrown away my life, my body, my soul —through this addiction. No longer will I allow food to fulfill a need or a void that only God can fulfill. I have been destroying God's sacred temple. Living a full, healthy life means making smart decisions every day. Each day of my life is made up of a variety of situations. In each situation, I have choices. I focus on selecting options that are right for me. I do not overindulge. I practice good portion control. I have a new love and respect for myself. I respect my body. I control food. Food no longer controls me. I easily and comfortably release that which I no longer need in life and I open myself up to You, God—have Your way.

SELF-ESTEEM

When God created the heavens and the earth, He looked at it and said that it was "good." As one of God's creations, we can rest assured that everything about us is "good." Unfortunately, many believers see themselves as unworthy or just not good enough.

BEAUTY IS IN THE EYE OF THE CREATOR

When God created the world, He had a master plan. He said that everything He touched was good. God doesn't do ugly. He only does beauty, and He does it on a grand scale. Beauty is God's fingerprint. When God created me, He created a person of beauty. I am His masterpiece, and I am a part of His master plan. God has His fingerprints all over me. I have been created by and touched by God. I am one of His children. I am beautiful. I dissolve every negative and false image of myself. I am whole and perfect, and my seeming imperfections are what make me beautiful. What seems imperfect to man is Your unique, creative design. I love who I am and am at peace with myself because I know that in the eyes of the Creator, I am beautiful.

GOD CLEANS UP MESS

When I make a mess of my life, God takes my mess and transforms it into His message of love. There is no limit to how good my life can become when I turn my life over to God completely.

TAKE THE LIMITS OFF

God I thank You, that You have given me unlimited potential. I have the privilege of being one of Your children, and I know that Your plan for my life is better than anything I can imagine. Limitations are not a part of that plan. Even if I have adopted limitations that seem to be written in stone, that is not a problem for You God. Your love can easily break them up and set me free. There is no limit to how good my life can become when I open my heart and mind to the power of Your love. You sent Your Son Jesus to change my expectations about what is possible. Until Jesus came, the blind, the poor, the prisoners, and the oppressed lived without hope. Jesus said that He came to announce good news to the poor, to proclaim freedom from the prisoners, to recover sight for the blind, to release the oppressed, to proclaim the year of the Lord's favor. Those are God's expectations for my life, and they are also my expectations. Good news, freedom, recovery, release from oppression and God's unlimited favor. There is no limit to how good my life can become when I live God's expectations for my life. No longer will I listen to the voice of limitation and fear because You designed me to fly like an eagle, and soaring is my domain.

GROWING HAIR

Father, because you know every fiber of hair on my head, my hair is growing longer and thicker day by day. Lord You promised that not a hair on my head shall perish. My hair is my crown of glory and power.

CHILDREN

Children face opposition and trials daily. They deal with temptation, crime, self-esteem and self-worth issues, bullying, peer pressures, uncertainty about their future and the list goes on. Thanks be unto God for He has promised to deliver our children and make them Disciples of Christ.

Read & Meditate: Psalm 127:3; Ecclesiastes 11:9; Isaiah 49:25 Amp; Proverbs 22:6; Isaiah 54:13; Psalm 112:2; John 10:27; Proverbs 3:5,6; Isaiah 44:2-4; Isaiah 61:9

CHILD IN TROUBLE

Father, I thank you for entrusting me with Your precious cargo—my child. Today I stand in the gap for (him/her). He/she has strayed from the path of righteousness and I ask that You deliver (him/her) from the hand of the enemy. The world says that I should let (him/her) make his/her own decisions and not invade on his/her privacy. That I should leave him/her be or I run the risk of losing my child forever. But the devil is a liar! Lord You see the assignment that has been perpetrated against him/her. I thank You that there are no difficulties in his/her life that You cannot conquer. It doesn't matter how deeply rooted the problem may be or how hopeless it may look. Father, Your Word declares that the seed of the righteous is delivered and I believe Your word is true. So therefore, I call (child's name) before You today and believe (child's name) is delivered. Establish Your Kingdom in him/her and remove every mountain that stands in his/her way. I will not accept the lies the evil enemy has planted in the life of my child-the lies that are all around him/her in the media, magazines, and at school. Lies that say it's okay to be promiscuous or it's cool to smoke, drink, and do drugs. Lies that say there's nothing wrong with sleeping with people of the same sex. Lies that say it's embarrassing to be a virgin. Lies that say it's not cool to go to church. Lies that say he/she has to get money at all costs because this is how they are defined. Lies that say it's okay to get tattoos or piercings even if it says "Jesus". Lies that tell him/her that he/she can escape the voices in his/her head by ending his/her life. All these lies are in direct opposition to Your Word. I annihilate all family curses. Lord place a hatred in him/her for sin and all that satan has to offer. I stand boldly today because I know that You are with (name of child). I know that You contend with him that contends with (name of child) and I declare that my child will live out Your plan for his/her life and not the plan of man. I have taught (name of child) in the way in which he/she shall go and I ask that You recall to their remembrance those things that he/she was taught and cause them to line up with Your word. Place Your hand upon him/her and keep him/her from evil. No weapons formed against my child will prosper; and tongues that rise against them shall be condemned-for this is the heritage of my child because (he/she) is a servant of the Lord.

PRAYER FOR CHILDREN

My children are the heritage of the Lord. Because I hunger and thirst for You O' God, I thank You that You pour Your Holy Spirit upon me and my children. I thank You God, that my children will be known among nations and their descendant among the peoples. All who see them will recognize and acknowledge that they are the people whom You have blessed. They are blessed in the city and in the fields. They are blessed when they come in and when they go out. Because we train our children in the way that they should go, and when they are old, they will continue to follow You and do what is right in Your sight. Allow them not to rush through life making decisions that could change God's plan for them. Right now in the Name of Jesus, we decree and declare that our children:

- Will find and fulfill the will of God for their life
- Are Spirit led and Holy Ghost filled
- Are willing and obedient and eat the good of the land
- Shall have the mates that God has chosen for them and will not be fooled by the devil's distractions
- Will not be overtaken by the lust and temptation
- Will have wealth and riches in their home
- Will consult God first before making any decisions
- Are protected against the enemy and no evil or plague will come near them
- Are taught of the Lord and great is their peace

- Are lenders, not borrowers and owe no man nothing but to love him
- Live long on the earth because they honor, obey, and respect us
- Continuously prosper and are in good health even as their soul prospers
- Fear God and exalt Him in every situation
- Are mighty seeds upon the earth
- Are upright and therefore shall be blessed
- Choose to hear the voice of the Good Shepherd and the stranger's voice they will not follow
- Are loving, giving, and compassionate showing God's mercy to others
- Are able to forgive those who wrong them so that they may remain in right standing with God
- Have the Spirit of Truth living in them and guiding them in all that is truth
- Have the mind of Christ and will not lean on their own understanding

Lord, I thank You that it is Your Will they grow and prosper in all things of the Spirit.

PROTECTION

There is no need for the believer to fear when trouble arises. God had promised in His Word to protect us.

Read & Meditate: Psalm 121:7; Proverbs 18:10; Psalm 121:2-3; Psalm 4:8; Psalm 91:10-11; Exodus 23:20; Ephesians 6:10; Isaiah 54:17; Deuteronomy 10:17-19; 1 Samuel 2:9

THE ALMIGHTY

O' Heavenly Father, JEHOVAH NISSI, my Father, the Most High God, are you not the Almighty? Have You not formed the entire world with Your voice? Do You not hold all power in Your hand? I say today let our God arise, and let His enemies be scattered. Who is able to withstand against You? Are you not Jehovah Nissi? El Shaddai? I shall fear no evil because You are with me and if You be for me, who can be against me? So I cover myself with the blood of my Lord and Savior Jesus Christ as my protection and surrender unto You. I take a stand against all the workings of satan that seek to kill me, steal from me, hinder me, and destroy me. Satan I command you, in the mighty name of Jesus to leave my presence and I claim the victory through Jesus Christ.

DRESSED TO KILL

I put on the whole armour of God that I may be able to stand against the wiles of the devil because you are our righteousness, Lord; the belt of truth and the shoes of the gospel of peace in which we stand, Lord Jesus Christ, because You are our truth and peace." "In my left hand I pick up the shield of faith, with which to quench EVERY fiery dart of the enemy, and place it in theirs, and decree by trusting faith that all of satan's plans are bound, we're loosed, and he is defeated in our lives this day and every day to come." "In my right hand I pick up the sword of the Spirit which is Your Word, Lord Jesus Christ and place it in theirs for Your Word says that no weapon formed against me shall prosper. I decree all these things accomplished in Your Name, Lord Jesus Christ, Amen." The shofar has blown and I declare that no weapon that is formed against me in this battle shall prosper. I am a servant of the Lord and this is my heritage.

AUTHORITY & IDENTITY

Read & Meditate: Genesis 1:27; Luke 10:19; Psalm 68:19; Isaiah 50:4; Malachi 3:17a NKJV; Isaiah 61:3; Ephesians 1:3, 4; Ephesians 2:10; Ephesians 3:6; Job 22:28; Hosea 4:6

I GOT THIS-AUTHORITY

I Got This! Lord, I thank You for the authority that You've given me in heaven and on earth. Because of the creative power invested in the Word of God, and because I have been created in Your image and likeness as a speaking spirit, I have the authority to speak to any situation that doesn't line up with the Word and command it to leave. I Got This! You have given me the tongue of those who are taught, that I may sustain with a word him that is weary. I Got This! I have been authorized to tread on all of the power of the enemy in the name of Jesus. I Got This! You load me daily with benefits. I Got This! I have been given everything that pertains to life and Godliness. Spirits of favor, counsel, might and power, come upon me, in the name of Jesus. I shall excel this day and nothing shall defile me. I shall possess the gates of my enemies.
 I Got This!

Inspired by First Lady Robin L. Burns of Jericho Church Without Walls

I AM THIS-IDENTITY

I am This! Father, I declare that I am beautiful and prosperous in Your sight. You think of me as a crown of glory and honor—the apple of Your eye—an exceedingly beautiful royal diadem—in Your hand. I am a jewel in Your Kingdom—Your workmanship, created in Christ Jesus for good works. I am Preordained, Predestined, Adopted, Accepted, Redeemed, and Forgiven. I am holy because God makes me holy. I am anointed to preach, teach, heal and cast out devils. I am a life changer. When I decree a thing, it is established in my life and in the lives of others. I have my sights set on excellence. I am a mighty force to be reckoned with. I am made in my Father's image. When I arise in the morning, demons shake and tremble because they know I am on assignment—I am about my Father's business. I am Kingdom-minded and purpose-driven. Many are destroyed for the lack of knowledge, but not me. I know who I am! My identity is sealed within me and cannot be stolen. I am motivated by the love and promises of God. I am a Partaker of the Promise. I am this!

Inspired by First Lady Robin L. Burns of Jericho Church Without Walls

GOVERNMENT

People don't typically pray for those who have decision making authority over them. They simply leave everything to chance when it comes to governmental affairs.

Read & Meditate: 1 Tim 2:2; Psalm 1:1; 1 Tim 2:2; Prov. 2:21-22; Prov. 2:11-12; Ps 25:21

GOD BLESS AMERICA
God, we ask that You shake up our government and cause them to be men and women of integrity, obedient concerning us. Let wisdom enter their hearts, and let knowledge be pleasant to them. Let discretion preserve them and understanding keep them. Cut off the wicked. Let the unfaithful be rooted out. Let the upright and blameless dwell and deliver them from the way of evil and from evil men. Keep them from abusing their offices and give them a virtuous accountability partner. I ask Lord, that the division that exists about how to solve the issues our country faces, would be abolished and that You will give a Spirit of unity. Surround us with favor among other countries and repair any damaged relationships.

NEIGHBORHOOD

Eight times in the Bible we are told to love our neighbor.

Read & Meditate: Galatians 5:14; Proverbs 3:29; Matthew 7:12; Romans 15:2; Romans 13:10; Proverbs 25:17-18; Leviticus 19:13

IT'S THE PLACE WHERE GOD LIVES

God rules and reigns in my neighborhood. The devil and all his forces cannot operate in my neighborhood because it is the place where God lives. I command you evil spirits who have been operating in my neighborhood, and blinding people to the Gospel of Jesus Christ, to come down from your place of illegitimate authority now in the Mighty Name of Jesus Christ. In Jesus' name my neighborhood is free from crime, gang activity, and illegal drugs. It is free from robbery, rape, kidnapping, perversion, and murder. People are turning away from their sins and seeking God like never before. Each and every neighbor loves and looks out for each other's safety and well-being. The adults and children in my neighborhood are serving in the local church and bringing others to Christ. People are being saved, healed, delivered, set free, transformed, and filled with the Holy Spirit every day because my neighborhood is the place where God lives.

OUR HOME

As for me and all that dwell in my house, we declare that we shall serve the Lord. We commit our home onto to You, Father; we deposit it into Your charge—entrusting those who dwell it in, and our possessions into Your care. We ask that You, by Your Holy Spirit use it for Your glory and honor. We plead the Blood of Jesus over our doorposts. We ask that anyone that steps foot into our home will not be able to resist Your Holy Spirit which is present throughout. If they came for evil, they will leave filled with Your Holy Spirit.

SETBACKS AND DISAPPOINTMENT

Life is full of setbacks and disappointments. It's not about WHAT you go through, but HOW you go through.

Read & Meditate: 2 Corinthians 4:8; 2 Corinthians 4:9; Psalm 34:7; Romans 8:28; Proverbs 24:16; John 5:8-9; Jeremiah 29:11

BACK IN THE GAME

I may have failed, but now I'm back in the game. I understand that the righteous may fall seven times but the key is he gets back up again. Never again will I let situations, circumstances, and conditions hold me down. Never again will I let setbacks and disappointments stop me from trying again. I will press, push, and pursue until I walk in victory. For I reflect on the victories You've given me in the past. I reflect on how You've brought me out. I know You haven't brought me this far to leave me alone. Father, I expect results because your Word does not return to You void in Jesus' Name. So with confidence in You, I can run this race knowing that the race is not given to the swift nor strong, but to me because I continue to Get Back in the Game!

MOVING FORWARD-STRATEGY

Many days, I find myself feeling over-worked and frustrated. But I avoid allowing these issues to negatively affect me. Whenever I experience stressful situations, I close my eyes briefly and remind myself that this is a part of life. I tell myself to stand strong, be courageous and walk out the situation because I know that God is with me. God is directing my life and will show me where to take the next step. I will keep moving forward until God says stop. I will act as if I cannot fail. I move in faith and I don't worry about what the future holds because God is already there waiting for me. I will act as if I cannot fail for as long as I have breath, and I will finish well. It won't be over until God says it's over. I'm moving forward.

TODAY IS THE DAY

I decree and declare that TODAY IS THE DAY! For, this is the day that the Lord has made. I know today, You have plans to prosper me and not to harm me, plans to give me hope and a future. I won't wait another day to walk in Your Will and the prosperity that You have preordained for me. TODAY IS THE DAY! It may not look like it. I may not feel like it, but I decree and declare that TODAY IS THE DAY! I might not know how to get out of my limitation, barrenness, sickness, debt, sorrow or loneliness but I feel it in my Spirit – My time has come! It's time to get up! Take up my bed and walk! Today is the Day!

OBEDIENCE

You can attend church every Sunday. You can lead Bible Study and teach Sunday school. You can even give to the poor every day, but if you are not walking in obedience, you will miss what God has for you. Obedience, simply put, is doing what you're told to do, when you're told to do it without hesitation. Obedience doesn't always feel good, but obedience is the path to blessings.

Read & Meditate: Matthew 7:21; Isaiah 1:19; Job 36:11; John 15:10; James 1:25; Deuteronomy 28:2; Ecclesiastes 5:7

WHATEVER YOU SAY

God I will move when You say move. I will press, push, and pursue and not look back. No more delay. No more hesitation. No more holding back. No more fear. No more compromise. I crucify my flesh and receive the blood of Jesus. Father, in the Name of Jesus, I break and destroy the spirit of procrastination and the spirit of fear that causes me not to be in full obedience to You. For now and forever more, I am walking in complete obedience to Your will. No more giving up. I press on toward the goal to win the prize that's in Christ Jesus. I am a doer of the Word. I will never give up or give in or get off track.

NOT MY WILL- I STEP OUT SO THAT YOU CAN STEP IN!

Lord, I foolishly tried to do things on my own. I now know that the creator of a thing has the right to define its purpose. Because You created me, I have no right to tell You what to do, how to do it, or even when to do it. I can only come into agreement with the plans and purposes that You already ordained for me before I was formed in my mother's womb. I don't want my own dreams and plans for the future to get in the way of what You have for me. Help me to see what You are up to. Do You want me to do something different from what I'm asking and seeking? Help me to trust You with the results. Because I know all things work together for the good of those who love and trust in You. Help me to see things in Your perspective and trust that You only desire the best for my life.

MAKING TOUGH DECISIONS/GUIDANCE & DIRECTION

Many times along life's path, we get lost and can't find our way. When we are in need of guidance, we can take pleasure in knowing that God will lead us along a path that will fulfill His plans for our life. He is the one who knows the direction you are to follow and will lead accordingly.

Read & Meditate: John 16:13; Proverbs 3:5-6; Psalm 31:3; Psalm 32:8; James 1:5; Psalm 32:8; Psalm 68:1; Isaiah 33:6; James 1:5; Ephesians 1:17

UPON YOUR WORD

Father, I know Your Word says that, "If any of you lacks wisdom, he should ask God, who gives generously to all without finding fault, and it will be given to him." So I come before You today asking You to guide me, instruct me and teach me in the way I should go. Father, I believe that the Spirit of Truth lives in me and You will guide me into all that is Truth. You will show me things to come as I allow You to speak into my life. Help me to trust in You with all my heart and lean not to my own understanding and in all my ways I will acknowledge You and You will direct my paths. Today I will hear Your voice, and I will not harden my heart as in rebellion. Make known to me Your thoughts and plans for my life. Give me the word of wisdom, knowledge, and prophetic utterance. I choose and thirst for Your voice. Guide me with Your counsel and let Your Words abide in me so that my ears will hear a word behind me saying, "This is the way, walk in it."

MORNING PRAYER

Father, I will rise and shine and give You the glory. I pray that now and through this day You will strengthen and enlighten me. Enable me to be the kind of person that pleases You. Forgive me for my sins both known and unknown. Create in me a clean heart and renew a right spirit within me. Do not cast me away from Your presence but allow me to stay near You. Let not my day be consumed with so much busyness that I miss all that You have prepared and provided for me this day. Let me not be so self-centered and consumed with my own issues and agenda that I forget to tell someone about You. Order my steps. Make them sure. Shut every wrong door and open every right door.

PASSING A TEST AT SCHOOL

Father, Your Word says that, if I lack wisdom, I can ask You and You will generously give it to me without reproach. I have an upcoming exam/assignment and I need Your help! Father, I have come to the place where I can no longer figure it out on my own. Give me the spirit of wisdom and revelation, and let the eyes of my understanding be enlightened. Call to my remembrance all that I have studied.

FINANCES-PROSPERITY

Although God wants to see us prospering, our motivation for prosperity cannot be to solely consume His blessings upon ourselves, but to realize, even as Abraham did, that we are blessed so that we can be a blessing. Please do a heart check before praying these prayers. Your motivation should be impacting the kingdom of God and changing the lives of others.

Read & Meditate: Psalm 72:12; Psalm 72:13; Psalm 68:10; Psalm 102:17; Psalm 113:7; Jeremiah 20:13; Psalm 112:3, 5, 9; Malachi 3:10-12; Haggai 1:6; Deuteronomy 8:7a, 9a; Philippians 4:19; Genesis 1:3,4; 1 John 5:14-15; John 14:14; Genesis 1:27

FINANCES

Thank You, Father, that because I am a tither, You are opening the windows of heaven and pouring me out such a bountiful blessing, that there is not room enough to receive it. You are rebuking the devourer for my sake. You will not destroy the fruits of my ground; neither shall my vine drop its fruit before the time in the field. All nations shall call me happy and blessed. Father, I declare that because I fear You, prosperity and welfare are in my house. It is well with me because I lend and deal generously. Because I have distributed freely and have given to the poor and needy, my righteousness endures forever and my horn shall be exalted in honor. I confess that every hole in my bag is closed. In the name of Jesus, I call in my resources from the east, the west, the north and the south. I command the earth to yield the fruit of my seed. I open the windows of heaven over my life to release the blessing because I am faithful in my tithes and offerings.

I WANT MY STUFF BACK!

In the name of Jesus, I loose myself and my lineage from all demonic forces that have taken away my money, possessions, and inheritance and cast them out into the abyss. I bind to me in Jesus' name promotions, business deals, raises, favor and all that is rightfully mine. I bind to myself every verse of the Bible that war against the demonic forces, and I violently and forcefully take back everything that the enemy has stolen from me. By the authority given to me by Jesus' shed Blood I render all of satan's plans and assignments null and void in my life and the lives of those I love. Spirit of Mammon, you have no right over my finances. God is my provider - He is the God of More than Enough. I serve God, I do not serve you. I deny you now. Mammon, I break your chains now over my thoughts and finances and you will go now under the feet of Jesus Christ according to Ephesians 1:22. Spirit of poverty, you have no right over my finances. You have kept me long enough in bondage. Satan take your hands off my stuff and your legs off my finances! The Bible says Jesus Christ came to give me a life of abundance. Sprit of poverty, I break your chains over my life and you will go under the feet of Jesus, and there I bind you with the truth of JESUS CHRIST. Go ministering angels and cause all imprisoned possessions and benefits to be released unto me now, in Jesus' Name. Let all blocked ways of prosperity be opened up now! I declare restoration 30, 60 and 100fold in Jesus' name. Lord, I boldly declare a million-fold blessing according to Genesis 24:60.

MONEY MAGNET

I am a Money Magnet! Money is attracted to me. I maintain my status as a Money Magnet because I am a giver. Even when it seems that I have given all that I had, money seems to find its way back to me. It flows in from the north, south, east, and west from multiple sources. People see me and just want to bless me. They may not understand why, but they are obedient. Money is freely available to me. Whatever I need, whenever I need it, wherever I need it, for as long as I need it, will always be at hand—effortlessly. I command an open heaven over my household. I command a 1000 fold return on every seed I've sown, every tithe and every offering. Every dollar I spend whether it be for food, mortgage, rent or bills come back to me multiplied. Father, I ask that You forgive me for any mismanagement of the money you entrusted me with.

BEING FRUITFUL

Open my blinded eyes Heavenly Father. I pray now that You would strengthen and enlighten me. Show me the ways in which satan is hindering me from receiving Your best. Show me his lies and distortion of the truth in my life. I choose not to be ignorant of his devices. I choose not to be conformed to satan and the ways of this world. I choose to be transformed by the renewing of my mind in Christ Jesus. I am as You created me to be. There is nothing missing, nothing lacking, and nothing broken. I am Your child and just as earthly children show characteristics of their parents, I am made in Your image. Come into my life, break down every idol, cast out every foe, and break up the weeds that are causing me not to bring forth fruit.

NEEDING FOOD

Thank You, Father, that You are bringing me into a good land— a land in which I shall eat food without shortage and lack nothing. I thank you Father for supplying all of my needs. Not based on what I have in the bank, but according to Your riches in glory in Christ Jesus.

LET THERE BE LIGHT

This is the confidence I have in approaching You Father and that is if I ask anything according to Your will, You hear me. And I know that because You hear me-- whatever I ask—You shall give to me. I know it's Your will God that I dwell in light. One of the first things You did when forming the earth was call forth Light. Therefore, by the power and authority given to me by Your Son Jesus and because I am made in Your image—I can speak in my situation and say, "Let There Be Light!" And I believe by faith that You are using someone with the power, ability, and influence to help my electricity be restored. Father, I repent for any misuse of the blessings that You have placed in my hands. Show me how to be a good steward over my finances so that I will never be in this situation again.

CONFUSION & DEPRESSION

Read & Meditate: 1 Peter 4:12-13; 1 Peter 5:7; Deuteronomy 31:8; Psalm 126:5; Psalm 34:18; Romans 15:13

CONTEMPLATING SUICIDE

Most gracious and forgiving God, I have to sought to end my life by my own hand. The pressure is too much and the burden feels so heavy. My thoughts and feelings have become overwhelming and I see no way out. I come today asking for Your forgiveness. I know that You have made a way of escape for me. Help me to courageously face each new day. Help me to see the light at the end of the tunnel. Thank You that when I feel I don't have any one to turn to, I can turn to You. You are a friend that sticks closer to me than a brother. When I am weak, You are strong. When I feel like giving up, You say keep pressing on. I plead the Blood of Jesus over my mind and I bind thoughts of suicide. I loose the same mind that is in Christ Jesus and the joy of living. God you are my Defender, the Master of my fate, and the Captain of my soul. You know my life from start to finish, and it won't be over until You say it's over. I have nothing to fear. I declare that I will live, not die and declare Your mighty works.

RESTORE MY MIND

Father, I apply the Blood of Jesus to my mind. I loose off me any spirit that would hinder me from hearing, reading, and memorizing Your Word, any spirits sent to bring confusion, scattered thoughts, forgetfulness, perverted thoughts, or any other destruction to me, in Jesus' name. I gather every loose spirit, bind them together and cast them into the abyss. I receive Jehovah-Shalom now.

BE YE TRANSFORMED

In order to have a new life, I need a new way of thinking. The Bible says, "Be transformed by the renewing of your mind." I can change my life by changing what I put into my mind. When I fill my mind with the God's words, His love and His promises, miraculous things happen. I need to think the way that God thinks. I need to get in agreement with God. I need to think abundance. I need to think possibility. I need to think forgiveness for myself and others. I need to think freedom from my past. I need to think release from my addictions. I need to think recovery from my sicknesses. I need to think about God's favor and love. I need to think the way God thinks. I have the mind of Christ. I declare that no negative thought shall manifest. I take them captive, I rebuke them, and I resist them in the mighty name of Jesus.

LOVE

God's love is not based upon meeting certain conditions. God's love is unconditional.

Read & Meditate: John 4:8

GOD'S LOVE COVERS

God created me, and He knows me better than I know myself. He knows what troubles and plagues me, and He has the cure. No matter what remedies I have tried in the past, if I have not experienced God's love, I am missing out on the most powerful medicine in the world. God's love always makes my life better. If I want my body to heal, an application of God's love will make it happen. If I want to restore wholeness to my heart and mind, I need to apply God's love. The most important fact in the universe is that God loves and accepts me the way I am, but He loves me too much to let me stay that way. When I fail, God's love never falters or fails. There is nothing that I can do to earn it. It will never stop pursuing me until the day I die. God's love surrounds and envelops me.

I HAVE A CLEAN SLATE

God loves me and accepts me the way I am, but He loves me too much to let me stay that way. That is my ultimate reason for hope. God is on my side. He wants to fill my heart with his love, banish my limitations, and wash away the plague of negative thoughts from my mind. God's love carries away my burden of guilt. His love not only wipes the slate clean, it also throws the slate away. God has a plan for my life that is better than anything I can imagine. There is no limit to how good my life can become when I receive and embrace the power of His love. The former things have passed away and I am new in Christ Jesus. I have a clean slate!

I LOVE ME SOME ME

I love me some me and I am deserving of all the good things in my life. Therefore, I deserve love! I am worthy of it. I first accept God's unconditional, unchanging love. Then I love myself so that others can freely love me.

GOD'S HOUSE

Amazing things happen when we as Believers come together and pray for our church and its leaders. When you take care of God's house, He will take care of yours.

Read & Meditate: Phil 4:2-3; Psalm 91:5-6; 11; Luke 10:19; Eph. 4:17; 32-5:1; Ps. 31:23; Ps 31:23; Prov. 28:20; Gal 6:9; Phil 1:6; Eph 2:10; Heb. 13:21; Heb. 13:2; Ps. 55:14; 119:63; 1 Thes. 5:17; Acts 1:14a; Mark 1:35; Matt. 4:10; Titus 2:4-5; Eph. 5:23-33; Heb. 12:15; Ps. 119:42; Col. 4:6; Prov. 31:26; 1 Pet. 2:23; Prov. 31:25a; 2 Cor. 5:20a; 1 Pet. 3:4; Isa. 54:13

GOD, HELP US!

Father, I cover my church, our pastor, his family, ministers, leaders, congregation, ministries, facilities, all that we are, have, and possess. Our families and children are blessed, our jobs are secure, our incomes come from multiple streams, finances are managed, and our bodies and all of our body parts and organs function the way that God intended. God, I pray that your church be unified in purpose and in love. I come against and destroy the roots of gossip, negative criticism, false expectations, unhealthy burdens, strife and weariness that will seek to invade our church family. God lock our hearts and minds as one to stand against the enemy. Keep those out of leadership who work on the basis of their own agendas and seek to sabotage the vision. Restore the joy of those church leaders who are serving without passion. Give us discernment to see what You desire. Teach us how to sow seeds of peace and harmony. Help us to resolve our differences lovingly, so that unbelievers would be drawn into Your family because of the love we share not the judgment that so many of Your "followers" claim is from you. Help us to be disciples who make disciples. Help us to love and be accepting of all who seek You!

CHURCH EMBARKING ON NEW BUILDING

In the name of Jesus, we shall decree a thing and it shall be established. We declare in Jesus' name that God ordained us prayer partners. God, You knew from the foundation of this world exactly what we needed and for that we say thank You. God, we declare that no weapon formed against us or our prayer life will prosper. God we pray right now for fuller manifestation of Your Holy Spirit to work in and rule over our lives, our family, our Man and Woman of God, our church family and the entire Body of Christ. We pray for a deeper connection with You, O' God. We come into agreement that (name of church)'s vision shall manifest to the fullest extent. In the name of Jesus, we thank You for favor in every area concerning our new building: favor with attorneys, the owners, funding sources (lenders as well as church members) and the community surrounding our new building. God, we realize that the things that are impossible with man are possible with You. Right now the things around us say it is not possible to purchase a building of this magnitude with the number of supporters we have, but thank you God, they are not our source. So we put our full trust in Your omnipotent power. We decree and declare that our new building will be a place of healing for the sick and brokenhearted; a place of deliverance for the lost and oppressed; a place of liberty for the captives; and a training ground for world changers. We thank you for the favor that you have released upon us with all people and that you keep adding to us daily those who are being saved from spiritual death.

PASTOR & HIS FAMILY

Pastor is referred to as "he" in this particular prayer because it was compiled for my pastor, Dr. Anthony D. Burns. If your pastor is a woman, feel free to change this pronoun to suit your Man or Woman of God.

Oh Father God, I pray for my pastor, for his family, for his marriage, and for his ministry. Watch over him and appoint Your angels to watch over his family as he watches over the flock. Cause them to abound with Your blessings. Lord, I thank You that Your ears are attentive to his prayers, and Your face is against those who plot evil against him. Direct him to lead resolutely, anchored on the rock of uncompromising faith. Make darkness light before him and crooked places straight. I pray that he will appropriate God's armor at all times to guard against the enemy's oppositions and attack. I tear down any stronghold over the pulpit. Give him the boldness to confront sin, church controllers, and evil spirits. Help him to set in order things that are lacking. Take him where You need him and work in him that which is well-pleasing in Your sight. Stir up his appetite for even more of You. As he spends time in the secret place, give him a renewal of his call. Release the fire of God that is in his belly and in his bones. Let that fire grow and engulf the flocks. Let the Word of God that he speaks be delivered in confidence with power, conviction, clarity, boldness, with love and in truth followed by signs and wonders. God, I pray that You will raise up people in this generation to use their power, ability, and influence to help my pastor carry out Your vision. And so I decree and declare that people with money will give money; that people with time will give time; that people with faith will exercise their faith; that people with big ideas and big dreams and big visions will give those ideas and dreams and visions to the ministry for Kingdom expansion. I pray that his family will never want or lack for anything as a result of him carrying out the vision. I call forth and thank You, God for co-laborers who are great thinkers, those who have teachable spirits and desire to work in love and unity as to the vision you have set forth. I command resources to flow into the various ministries under his leadership because it is Your work and what You have purposed to be done. I declare that money will overflow into his personal bank account for his household. Give him opportunities and finances to take enough time away from ministry so that he doesn't get worn out. Let him never get weary in well doing but allow him to look for the favor as he moves forward. Reveal the deeper things of God to him by Your spirit. I command all blessings to come upon him now and overtake him because he obeys the voice of the Lord. I declare that every place the soles of his feet tread upon has been given to him. God birth the things you have spoken to him in his heart. Preserve him through whatever trial is facing. Father, forgive me for any times that I may have caused him to grieve. Teach me how to encourage him.

THE FIRST LADY (PASTOR'S WIFE)

God bring godly friends and encouragers to my First Lady and her family, to strengthen her for the ministry and to provide meaningful fellowship, accountability, and times of rest. I thank You that she is a woman of prayer and worship, and that she leads by example—teaching us how to walk in a close relationship with the Father. I thank You for her strong character and uncompromising integrity. Protect her marriage and keep it strong as a model of the Church's submission to Christ. I thank

You that she respects and practices godly submission to her husband's leadership, and that her husband loves and cherishes her openly and in private. I thank You that he sees her as "a good thing" which allows them to obtain favor from God! I sprinkle the Blood of Jesus over their family time that it will be protected and sacred. Lord, never let the pressures of the ministry discourage or embitter her or her children. Protect her from discouragement and bitterness when she or Pastor faces inevitable criticism. I thank You that the wisdom of the Word of God answers her critics, and she commits herself into the hands of God, who judges righteously. I declare that any and all "gossipers" that may be acting as agents of divisiveness concerning their marriage be SHUT UP AND SHUT DOWN COMPLETELY concerning the matter. Lord, cloth her with strength and dignity. I thank You for her gentle and gracious spirit. We shun any notion that she must play a role, maintain a certain image, or be the perfect wife, mother, and Christian just because she is the Pastor's wife. But we declare that she is a great ambassador of Your love, Your kindness, Your forgiveness, and You mercy and ministry flows from her effortlessly. I thank You, Lord that she loves the women of the church as her own daughters—training and building us up to minister in the church and in our own homes.

YOUR DAUGHTERS IN MINISTRY

Lord Jesus, You have redeemed us and made us Your precious daughters. Father, You have a divine purpose and design for everything. Rain gives water to the earth and bringing forth life. Just as You've made rain for a purpose, Father, we know You made us, Your daughters, on and for a purpose. This, we are certain. We are here on purpose for You, to do Your Will. Our desire is to please You, to follow You and do whatever it is that You purposed for us to do. Lord help us to see that which You desire for us in ministry. God, as women, we have so many talents and skills and You know, Lord, that we will jump in anywhere to make it happen. But today Lord, we want what You want for us. We empty ourselves and ask You to fill us with the full power of your Spirit. Help us surrender ourselves to you completely. Fill us with the glory of Your presence and by Your hand, we will walk boldly today where You lead us, carrying Your light in this dark world. Our mind is open, our heart is willing. We only hear, see, do and speak what is pleasing to You. We declare that we are not what and who the world thinks we are. We are who and what You ordained us to be. We are strong and we are mighty in Your Kingdom. We thank You that we carry life in our wombs and our mouths. Father, thank You for calling us also to be prophetic intercessors speaking life to our husbands, sons, daughters, friends, and family. We praise You that You release the counsel of your will to us so that we are not ensnared by the enemy's trap. Father, Your Word declares that there is neither Jew nor Greek, there is neither slave nor free, there is no male and female, for we are all one in Christ Jesus. We destroy any religious spirits that have been holding Your daughters back. We thank You for Jesus who affirmed the equality of women in the midst of a culture that denied us basic human rights. He called them to be His disciples during a time when religious leaders taught that it was disgraceful even to teach a woman. Father, we thank You for the great example of both old and new testament women who served You. We thank You for Esther, Deborah, Phoebe, Priscilla, and even Phillip's daughters. Thousands of years later, many of Your daughters are still fighting to serve You in their true calling. But Father, today, we declare that winds of opposition will not frustrate what You have placed on the inside of us. We declare that erroneous teachings and doctrines will not hold us. We will move forward in Your timing and in Your divine order. Daughters thou art loose and we bind to us is the Spirit of Truth. We are in a prophetic hour and we declare that the set time for us to walk in that Truth is now! Our set time for promotion is now! We prophesy the great outpouring of Your spirit upon Your daughters both young and old. We call forth the Apostles, Prophets, Evangelists, Pastors, Teachers, the Prayer Warriors, the Psalmists, the Musicians, the Watchmen, the Gatekeepers, the Authors, the Giant Killers, and the Demon Slayers...We call them to do the work of the Kingdom. We call them to stand up in this hour and declare Your Word and do Your Works in the local ministry. We thank You God that You've called us from our hiding places, from our comfort zones, and even out of fear for such a time as this. We thank You for the presence of Your Holy Spirit for manifold equipping to see who we are in You and to understand our assignment. Make us the army of watchmen in this season so that we may rise up and take our positions in the earth now…with great strength. Let your anointing fall mightily upon your daughters as we do Kingdom work. Teach us how to lead, but give us the grace to be even better servants. God we declare that we are women of the Book, who love and study and obey the Bible in every area of its teaching; that meditation on biblical truth is the source of hope and faith; that we continue to grow in understanding through all the chapters of our lives. God make us women of prayer, so that Your Word will be opened to us, and so the power of faith and holiness will descend upon us; so that our spiritual influence may increase at home and at church and in the world. God we declare that we serve our Pastor and First Lady like our very lives and prosperity depends on it…because it does. We are submitted and obedient. "Father, show us our heart the way You see it. Reveal to us all that is unholy in us, all unholy actions, behaviors, habits, thoughts, and beliefs; all that keeps us from drawing closer to You and from serving You to the fullest. Holy Spirit, by the scalpel of Your Word and the Blood of Jesus, do Your operation on us through our faith in Jesus. (Col.2:12) Apply your knife of the work of the cross to our "flesh' and the soul-life that agrees with it, in a steady and persistent manner. Be relentless, Holy Spirit. Cut out all pride, stubbornness, secret pride, secret sin, presumption, ambition, and all that is of self. self-will, self-promotion, self-indulgence, all desires for self-gratification or self-aggrandizement, all ministry rooted in "self" and "self-promotion", all unholy habits and appetites, all sins of the tongue, sins of the heart, sins of the flesh; the lust of the eye, lust of the "flesh", and pride of life. Get us out of the world, Lord, and get the world out of us. All in Your Name and for Your Glory, Lord Jesus Christ, Amen."

RELATIONSHIPS

God didn't create us to go at it alone, however, we must discern what relationships we need to maintain and which ones we need to move away from.

Read & Meditate: Philippians 2:2; 1 Corinthians 1:1; John 13:34-35; Ephesians 4:32; 1 Peter 1:22; 1 Corinthians 1:10

BROKEN RELATIONSHIP

Father, I know that You are a God of restoration. I come to You asking not for restoration of the relationship for I desire for Your Will to be done in my life, but asking for restoration and wholeness in my being. I refuse to waste time on regret. I trust You with my heart and I lift my heart to You and ask that You fill me with Your love. Your unconditional, unfailing love that never leaves me feeling lost or in pain. Help me to not follow my emotions, but show me how to lead my emotions. Restore my joy. Anyone or anything you do not want in my life, allow them to leave and stay gone. Allow me to let it go.

FAVOR

God wants to favor you today. This promise can be found in Isaiah 30:18.

Read & Meditate: Genesis 39:3–4; Psalm 5:12; Psalm 23:5–6; Numbers 6:25–26; Psalm 8:4–6; Acts 2:46–47; Romans 6:14; Hebrews 4:16; Job 10:12; Job 33:26; Psalm 30:5; Psalm 44:3 Psalm 41:11; Psalm 89:17; Psalm 102:13; Psalm 106:4; Proverbs 3:3-4; Proverbs 8:32-35; Proverbs 11:27; Proverbs 12:2; Proverbs 14:9; Proverbs 18:22; Proverbs 28:23; Isaiah 45:2-3; Isaiah 60:10; 1 Samuel 2:26; Luke 2:52; Luke 2:13-14

THANK YOU FOR FAVOR

Lord, Thank You that I have favor with You and man today. All day long, people go out of their way to bless and help me. When people approach me, the first thing they come into contact with is my favor shield. I thank You, Heavenly Father for opening doors for me that neither man nor the devil can shut. I want to thank you for causing me to be at the right place at the right time. I want to thank you for causing people to want to help me.

RECEIVING FAVOR

God, There are times when I pushed away the good things that came to me, such as compliments, gifts, recognition or payments for my work. I am learning that when I deprive myself and reject what comes to me, I am denying You and refusing the abundance You are giving me. You are the Source and Giver of everything. Please help me to feel worthy of receiving, enjoying and celebrating all good things that come to me, without resistance. I choose to honor You by receiving Your gifts with unwavering joy and gratitude. Each time I receive the blessing of someone's gift, time, money or love, I am honoring You, myself and also the person who You touched to be a blessing to me. The greatest thing I can do to help others is to first receive what You have given and then extend Your gifts of love and abundance into the world as I have received them. This infinite circle of receiving what You have given and then giving as we have received ensures our ever-expanding growth. Thy will be done. Amen

MY WORDS

Words are powerful. Words can start wars. Lives are shattered in an instant by words. Words create. Words give life. Words judge. It is important that we understand the power of words.

Read & Meditate: Ecclesiastes 12:11, Hebrews 1:3, Ezekiel 37:4-7; 9-10; Jeremiah 1:9

I am an imitator of Jesus, the Master Builder, the God who created the world and the fullness thereof with His words. My words are powerful. Death and life are in the power of my tongue, and I choose life. Therefore, I will not let any corrupt communication proceed out of my mouth. I speak only those things that cause God's will to manifest on earth. I speak to situations and they have no choice but to change.

SUCCESS

Good News! As a child of God, you have been authorized to succeed in life.

Read & Meditate: John 4:8

CONFIDENCE IN GOD'S PLAN

As long as I believe in God and obey His Word, my life continues to move forward in positive ways. When I have confidence in Jesus, I am free. There's no need to depend on or cling to others because I know I am successful and can do all things through Jesus Christ who gives me the strength to take on any and every challenge. I trust that I have the power that God has placed within me to do whatever is necessary to have a good life. Today, I am sure I can handle any challenges that may arise. I focus on making each of minute of my life count. I embrace everything positive that comes my way as I release everything else. I am confident about my future success because I follow God's plan for my life.

I HAVE THE ANSWER

Because I strive to be financially fit and responsible, I keep my eyes open to any new business prospects and ideas that might come along. I don't let difficulties discourage me because I know that in the middle of every difficulty lies opportunity. I want to be prepared to benefit for opportunities that God sends my way to increase my income whenever they arrive. I strive to be ready for any chance to do business with others. Therefore, I invest in myself by reading books, attending seminars, taking classes, and seeking out Godly mentors. When an opportunity presents itself, I seek God first. Then and only then, I make a decision. I try to find a time in each day when I can achieve something, regardless of how small. I intend to focus my efforts on doing something little each day that brings me closer to attaining my business's goals. What the world needs and desires, I am ready to produce and give.

MY BELIEF DETERMINES MY DESTINY

My beliefs about myself determine my level of confidence. Whether I am beginning a new project, attending a social event, or experiencing changes in a personal relationship, how my life progresses is largely determined by what I believe. I am blessed with the power to change how I see things. Father, help me to let go of false beliefs and embrace Your Word.

UNSTOPPABLE

God has given me great vision; a vision that will ultimately impact and change the world forever. With Him, I am Invincible. I know where I am going and the world steps aside for me. I am immune to the words "no", "stop", and "give up". Obstacles do not intimidate me because I rise boldly and courageously to challenges. My gifts and talents will make room for me in a way that no man can deny. I am unstoppable!

Salvation

Jesus Christ came to disturb the world, and to turn the lives of humankind to God. Not only did He bring love to those who were unloved, hope to those who had nothing to look forward to and peace to those who were full of anxious daily cares, but He also brought judgment to those who thought they were good, to those who were content with their own lives, to those who looked down on other people and who were sure that they knew everything about God. Most importantly, He brought life to those who were destined for hell.

Read & Meditate: Romans 10:9-13; John 3:3; 2 Peter 3:9; 1Timothy 2:4; 2 Corinthians 4:3,4; Ephesians 6:12

PAYER FOR SALVATION

Father, I know that I have broken Your laws and my sins have separated me from You. I am truly sorry, and now I want to turn away from my past sinful life toward You. Please forgive me, and help me avoid sinning again. I believe that Your son, Jesus Christ died for my sins, was resurrected from the dead, is alive, and hears my prayer. I invite Jesus to become the Lord of my life, to rule and reign in my heart from this day forward. Please send Your Holy Spirit to help me obey You, and to do Your will for the rest of my life. In Jesus' name I pray, Amen."

After you have confessed this prayer out loud, please e-mail me at: **sfifer@strengthtoendure.org**. I want to celebrate with you and send words of encouragement to help you along your journey.

NOT READY TO RECEIVE SALVATION

Heavenly Father, I come to You and ask You in Jesus' name to set me free from any wrong thoughts, fear, doubt, unbelief, believing any lies, any lies of the enemy, the devil, or demonic spirits, and any thoughts that I have that are hindering me now in coming to You. I ask You, Father God, to deliver me now of all hindrances to becoming Your born-again Kingdom child, in Jesus Christ's Holy name. I resist the devil and all his demonic spirits must flee and leave my presence. Lord God, remove the lies and the hindrances and help me so I can say the above prayer of salvation in earnest from my heart! I ask You to force out, drive out, and bind all evil things far away from me, in Jesus' name. Amen.

References

I cannot take full credit for putting together all of these prayers and confessions. Parts of it were taken from the Bible, sermons, other prayer books, and websites that I have read and studied over the years. Unfortunately, I do not remember all of the resources to give them proper credit. Below is my attempt to honor those sources.

Burns, A. & R. (2012). *With this Ring.* Overflow Publishing. Milwaukee, WI

Burns, A. (2006) Maximizing the Power of Agreement. Sermon Series, A.D. Burns Ministries, Milwaukee, WI

Goodman, E. (2004). Passion Prayer of Jesus Christ.ebook.

Kirk, P. (2008). *At the Last Supper, did Jesus know he would rise again?* Retrieved on December 27, 2012, from http://www.gentlewisdom.org/442/at-the-last-supper-did-jesus-know-he-would-rise-again/

Sheets, D. (2006). *Authority in Prayer. Praying with Power and Purpose.* Bethany House Publishing. Grand Rapids, MI

Zunpano, B. (1999). *Spiritual Warfare Prayers.* Oral Roberts University School of Medicine, Tulsa, Oklahoma. Harbor Light Publishers.

ACKNOWLEDGMENTS

I have been blessed with a **husband, Rodney** who understands and supports my artistic endeavors (even the weird, embarrassing stuff). I thank you for your encouragement and enduring this process without complaint. I know if no one else in the world prays for me, you will. Love ya! No one can compare.

Then to my **children, Diante, Traneisha, Trashiva, Triana, Tyja, Donavan, Darius, Rodney Jr., and Dimitri**, whose unconditional love for me keeps me pressing, pushing, and pursuing God's best so you won't have to work that hard. I love you more than you will ever know. You are my precious gifts from God and this is my attempt to leave a legacy of excellence for you and generations to come. Man, you are the best kids a mother can ask for. You are constant reminders of God's favor on my life.

To my **mother, Theresea Houston**, thank you for training me up in the way in which I should go. All that you instilled in me never departed. You laid the foundation. I love you!

Dr. Anthony D. Burns, my Pastor, my Father, my Life Coach, my Spiritual Cut-man- where and who would I be if God hadn't led my family to Jericho Church? As I wrote this book, I constantly heard your voice saying, "Stay focused!" "Keep pressing!" "It's already on the inside of you!" Dr. Burns, you are definitely one who truly made a difference in my life. It was under your tutelage that I developed a focus and became interested in vision, my purpose and manifesting the things of God. I asked God for success for four simple reasons: 1) so that He (God) can get the glory. 2) So I can be a blessing to others. 3) So I can meet all of my family's needs and desires. And last, but certainly not least, 4) So that you can know that everything you poured in me was not in vain. P.S. Thank you for most of the material in this book. LOL!

First Lady Robin L. Burns, my Spiritual Mother, from the beginning, you embraced me. I thank you for your inspiration. I am a better wife, mother, and person because of the example you set. I doubt that I will ever be able to convey my appreciation fully, but I owe you my eternal gratitude. Thanks for taking time out of your busy schedule to be my editor.

Min. Nina Haliburton and the Jericho Intercessory Prayer Team: Min. Simone, Min. Brumfield, Min. Latreeta, Min. Mark, Min. Eferin, and Min. Brenda, and my Personal Prayer Eagle: Min. Millicent. Thanks goes out to each of you. You have been great examples to me. You guys provided me with advice, encouragement, and prayer at times of critical need. Priceless!

ABOUT THE AUTHOR

Sharan Fifer is an anointed vessel of God who has been called to the Kingdom for such a time as this. She has a passionate love and deep hunger for the Word of God coupled with a love for God's people. Sharan strongly believes in the power of prayer, obedience, and unity in the Body of Christ. Sharan is the daughter of the late, Reverend Grover Woodfork.

Raised in a Christian home, her mother always pressed into her the importance of prayer. She wandered from the church during her teen years and found herself searching for fulfillment in relationships, personal achievement and material things. Through it all she never wondered away from prayer.

In 2006, a burning, intense fire ignited in her when she became a member of Jericho Church Without Walls in Milwaukee, WI. There she developed a hunger for more and more of God. It was at Jericho that she received her PhD (POWER, HEALING, AND DELIVERANCE). In 2007, after surrendering to God's will, she answered the call to ministry. Under the guidance and leadership of her spiritual parents, Dr. Anthony D. Burns and First Lady Robin L. Burns, Sharan enrolled in Jericho's Minister Training and Development Institute. The intense training offered helped her propel forward into the Kingdom of God to fulfill her God-given destiny.

She has served in many areas of the ministry such as Sunday school teacher, small group facilitator, choir member, and fellowship manager and now serves as an Intercessor on the Next Level Prayer Team and under First Lady Robin L. Burns in the Women of Excellence Ministry. Sharan Fifer is also a certified Master Life and Business Success Coach. Her formal training is in Organizational Management from Ashford University in Clinton, IA. While sharing her own struggles, failures, and successes Sharan is known for her humorous and poignant anecdotes that keep others laughing, crying, and examining their own lives. Her passion is to encourage women to renew their minds through God's word that they may live transformed lives.

Sharan is first and foremost a wife and mother. She resides in Milwaukee, WI with her husband, Minister Rodney L. Fifer, Sr. and their beautiful children, who also have an intense love of God.

Recommended Books

With this Ring, Authors Anthony D. Burns & Robin L. Burns

It's All About the Children, Author Robin L. Burns

I'm So Satisfied and *Better Believe God*, Author Nina Halliburton

A Place of Refreshing, Author Sharon Brumfield

Passion Prayer of Jesus, Author Elisha Goodman

Pigs in the Parlor, Author Frank and Ida Mae Hammond

They Shall Expel Demons, Author Derek Prince

Let Us Pray Together Now! A Spiritual Warfare and Prayer Guide, Author Angie Ray

Prayers that Rout Demons, Author Apostle John Eckhardt

Prayers that Bring Change, Author Apostle Kimberly Daniels

www.ingramcontent.com/pod-product-compliance
Lightning Source LLC
Chambersburg PA
CBHW060510030426
42337CB00015B/1827